25 Mountain Bike Tours
in Vermont

25 Mountain Bike Tours
in Vermont

**Scenic Tours Along Dirt Roads, Forest
Trails, and Forgotten Byways**

William J. Busha

Photographs by the author

A 25 Mountain Bike Tours™ Guide

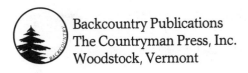

Backcountry Publications
The Countryman Press, Inc.
Woodstock, Vermont

An Invitation to the Reader

Although it is unlikely that the roads you cycle on these tours will change much with time, some road signs, landmarks, and other items may. If you find that changes have occurred on these routes, please let us know so we may correct future editions. The author and publisher also welcome other comments and suggestions. Address all correspondence to:

Editor
25 Mountain Bike Tours™ Series
Backcountry Publications, Inc.
P.O. Box 175
Woodstock, Vermont 05091

Library of Congress Cataloging-in-Publication Data

Busha, William, 1948–
    25 mountain bike tours in Vermont: scenic tours along dirt roads,
forest trails, and forgotten byways/William J. Busha; photographs
by the author.
      p.   cm.
   "A 25 mountain bike tours guide."
   ISBN 0-88150-130-1
   1. All-terrain cycling – Vermont – Guide-books. 2. Vermont-
-Description and travel – 1981- – Guide-books. I. Title.
II. Title: Twenty-five mountain bike tours in Vermont.
GV1056.B87   1989
917.43 – dc20   89–32132
                                                   CIP

Published by Backcountry Publications
A division of The Countryman Press, Inc.
Woodstock, Vermont 05091

Printed in the United States of America
Typesetting by Sant Bani Press
Cover design by VLS Designs
Text design by Richard Widhu
Maps by Richard Widhu, © 1989 Backcountry Publications

Cover photograph courtesy of Vermont Mountain Bike Tours
in Pittsfield, Vermont 05762

Photograph on page 55 courtesy of the Vermont Historical Society

Acknowledgements

I am indebted to several people for their help in completing this book. I wish to thank my publisher, Carl Taylor, for his guidance as this book evolved, Jane McGraw for her skillful editing of the manuscript, and Jeanie Levitan for producing the finished product. I am grateful to my sons Daniel and Peter for sharing with me their unflagging enthusiasm for backroad excursions, and I reserve special thanks for my wife Jo, whose encouragement and support made it possible for me to research these trips.

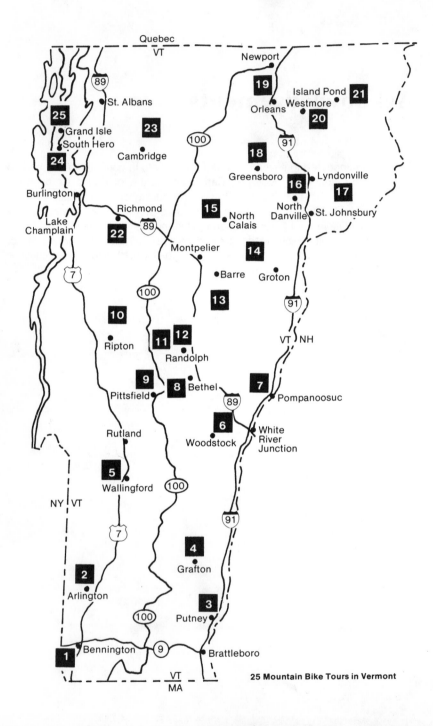

25 Mountain Bike Tours in Vermont

Contents

Vermont byways are scenic and lightly traveled.

Introduction

Welcome to the Real Vermont

Vermont might well have been created as a model of the ideal mountain bike environment. Its very name (from the French "verde mont," meaning "green mountains") conjures up an accurate image of abrupt, forested peaks; panoramic vistas; rushing streams; and remote byways.

Vermont is one of the most heavily forested states in the country, with about seventy-five percent of the land covered with trees. It is also one of the most rural, with its three largest cities containing only sixty, thirty, and twenty thousand people respectively. The remaining population of less than a half million is spread out over nearly ten thousand square miles.

The first settlers arrived in Vermont more than two hundred years ago and established bustling, self-sufficient communities in the hills. Many of the early communities eventually declined, and new ones developed, as migration to western lands, the coming of the railroads, and the interstate highway system dictated demographic changes.

Although the people may have relocated and their old houses become cellar holes, the transportation network that connected these communities has remained, a network perfect for backroad bicycling — miles and miles of unpaved roads and trails. There are nearly fourteen thousand miles of roads in Vermont, and more than half of them are unpaved. There are hundreds of additional miles of forest byways accessible only to four-wheel-drive vehicles, as well as logging roads and snowmobile trails that offer excellent mountain bike riding.

And best of all, all this is still a well-kept secret. Although Vermont has become one of the most popular destinations for bicycle tourists in the last fifteen years, this riding has been done almost exclusively on pavement and has been restricted to the areas accessible to motorists. On a mountain bike in Vermont, you can take the road less traveled and enjoy the state's natural beauty on a more intimate level.

The lure of the backcountry has drawn a select minority of Vermont cyclists for decades. Writing in the 1942 "Middlebury College Newsletter," student bicyclist David Wood points out that "all roads are bike roads, whether they be uphill (in many cases) or downhill, whether they be dirt roads overgrown with weeds, black tops, or smooth macadam.

You'll see the most . . . if you stick to the first kind, a little less if you take to black tops, and if you follow the very beaten path, you'll see what everybody else sees."

Ten years later, Collamer Abbott made a similar discovery and reported it to readers of the summer 1953 issue of *Vermont Life.*

At first glance the country roads that crisscross Vermont seem too formidable for the lowly bicyclist who has to furnish his own motive power. But if you like to take scenery in leisurely doses and don't mind walking a little, cycling can open new vistas.

After four years of riding over dirt roads . . . I . . . [became] convinced that the "real" Vermont is far from the "traffic crowded" main highways and can be enjoyed most from a bicycle.

Planning a Trip

The Routes. The routes described in this book have been loosely grouped into regions, and each tour includes a listing of nearby accommodations. For the most part, the trips in a given region are close enough together so that you can do any of them while staying at the same lodging establishment. In addition, there will be back roads and trails near every place of lodging that you can explore on your own. Always make reservations in advance, particularly during the foliage season or around holidays.

The Season. Cycling season in Vermont begins around the first of May. Earlier than that, many dirt roads are too muddy, and snow may still cover forest trails. Such conditions may exist in some places even in May. Riding tapers off in the fall when it starts to get cold, or when it snows, usually in late October. Hunting is a popular fall sport, and it's a good idea to wear some fluorescent orange for safety if you ride then. This is particularly true during deer hunting season, which begins in October for bow hunters and continues into November for rifle hunters. Although the tours in this book do not address winter riding, that too is possible on dirt roads under the right conditions—normally when the temperature is 35° or above and the road is well-sanded or has no underlying layer of ice.

Before Leaving. Prior to leaving on a trip, read the description in its entirety. Then make a photocopy of the pages and bring the copy with you. Pack a lunch, for you may ride for several hours without passing a store. Other things you may want to bring are a camera, a compass, and a compact fishing outfit.

Recommended Equipment

The Bike. You will need a mountain bike, preferably one with eighteen speeds and fat tires. Some bicycles sold as mountain bikes come from the factory equipped for an urban market and city riding and

More than one hundred covered bridges are still in use in Vermont.

may have only twelve or even ten speeds and thinner tires. For riding the Vermont backcountry, tires of a two-inch size or greater are desirable.

Odometer. You will find the directions easier to follow if you have one of these, since cumulative mileage points are used for reference. You can probably complete the trips without an odometer, using the maps and your own intuitive sense of distance, but this risk will increase your chances of getting lost.

Buy an odometer with increments to a tenth of a mile. There are several good ones on the market, some for under thirty dollars. Some models are difficult to mount to a mountain bike's fatter tubes. If the mounting hardware is not sized for a mountain bike, your dealer will have to mount it using a customized bracket.

Tool Kit. Carry the tools just in case. Many of these routes truly are "miles from nowhere," and it's best to be prepared. For tire repair, be sure to include tire irons, a patch kit, and a pump, and be familiar with the procedure for repairing flats.

Hard riding can loosen bolts, and a selection of wrenches can spare you a frustrating experience. On one summer ride, I was about four miles into the woods when I landed hard on the saddle after an unexpected bump. The jar was enough to loosen the bolt that controls the saddle's position so that it flopped uselessly up and down and from side to side. A simple turn of the wrench would have solved the problem, but when I reached for the tools, I remembered that they were with my son's bike, many miles away. Riding a bike standing up is useful for climbing hills, but I don't recommend it for extended trips.

Include both standard and Phillips screwdrivers, a selection of wrenches in sizes from eight to eleven millimeters and Allen wrenches in four, five, and six millimeter sizes.

Chain Tool. I haven't had a problem with the chain on my bike yet, but one bike shop owner told me of several cases he has seen. Apparently, sticks extending into the trail can catch on the derailleur and snap it in two, leaving you with no way to tighten the chain. With a chain tool, you can remove an eight- to ten-inch section (or whatever is needed) and convert the bike to a one-speed that will allow you to limp back to the starting point. Not perfect, but it beats walking.

Extra spokes, a spoke wrench, and spare cables for both brakes and gears complete the selection of repair equipment you'll need to make most emergency repairs.

Pack. Some kind of pack will be needed to carry supplies. I like the type that mounts on a rear rack, although the handlebar-mounted packs with a clear plastic pocket for a map or tour directions are handy.

Dog repellant. Domestic dogs can be a problem, particularly on farms located on the remote back roads. Many are tied, but some are not. Outrun them if you can. If that's not possible, reach for your can of Halt; I never ride without a container of it and keep it clipped to my belt where it's readily available.

Insect repellant. Consider packing some. Vermont's verdant forests produce a healthy crop of insects each year, and they tend to bother some people more than others. For example, I have read that different black flies prefer to feed on different hosts and may travel as much as fifty miles to find the host they desire. That may partly explain why one person can receive many more bites than another, a phenomenon that I have witnessed more than once in wilderness settings, although clothing color and cosmetic scents play a part as well.

Although the pattern varies in different parts of the state, generally in the first third of the summer black flies are the greatest problem; in the middle third, mosquitoes take over; and for the last third, deer and horse flies predominate. I find this last group to be the biggest nuisance because they readily pursue a moving object.

Clothing. Dress in layers, preferably in wool. A vigorous climb up one side of a mountain will make you sweat profusely, and a rapid descent down the other side will chill you uncomfortably. Plus, daily temperatures in Vermont can rise and fall quite dramatically, especially in the spring and fall.

Water. Carry your own drinking water. Most Vermont streams look pure enough to drink, and many are, but they sometimes carry impurities. A rotting deer carcass or a giardia-infected beaver colony may be just upstream.

Reflective material. Use reflective tape, legbands, or clothing that includes reflective material when riding at dusk. Some of the trips in this book take several hours and conclude on well-traveled roads.

Safety

Unfortunately, thousands of bicycle accidents occur every year and have been happening for a long time. Consider the warning of a Baltimore preacher who assailed his congregation from the pulpit nearly one hundred years ago:

> These bladder wheeled bicycles are diabolical devices of the demon of the darkness. They are contrivances to trap the feet of the unwary and skin the nose of the innocent. They are full of guile and deceit. When you think you have broken one to ride and subdued its wild and satanic nature, behold it bucketh you off in the road and teareth a great hole in your pants. Trust not the bike when it bloweth upon its wheels, for at last it bucketh like a bronco and hurteth like thunder. Who hath skinned legs? Who hath a skinned nose? Who hath ripped breeches? He that dallies along with the bicycle. (From *A Social History of the Bicycle*, by Robert A. Smith, American Heritage Press, 1978)

Although these well-intentioned remarks may seem humorous at a century's distance, the subject is a serious one. Safety experts claim that a thousand people a year die from head injuries alone in bicycling accidents. Many of the deaths could have been prevented if the riders had been wearing helmets, and you should never ride without one.

Some hazardous situations occur more frequently than others on the trail. Riding over slippery wet logs or rocks that are not perfectly flat can pitch you sideways. Riding in a rut and having the pedal hit the ground can also throw you, and failure to keep your weight well in back of the saddle, combined with too much pressure on the front brake, will pitch you over the handlebars.

Wild animals abound in Vermont and should be left alone. Don't feed them, and be particularly suspicious if they seem unafraid of you. Male moose might view you as a competitor during the fall rutting season, so if you are lucky enough to see one, keep your distance. Black bears will most likely run from you, but conventional outdoor wisdom says not to come between the mother and the cubs. I know from experience that this rule is easy to forget in the excitement of coming upon one of these shy bruins.

Vermont is blessed with plenty of cool, peaceful picnic spots.

One of the great things about backroad cycling is the absence of traffic, particularly if you ride on a weekday. However, you will encounter some cars and trucks, and it's important to remember that the surprise element may be more of a factor here than on paved roads. Many drivers are not expecting to see bicyclists on back roads.

Preferably ride with another person. If you ride alone, make sure someone knows where you are planning to ride. Some of the areas you will pass through on these trips may not be visited by another person for days, so you can't count on help from passersby if you have a problem.

Allow plenty of time to complete a trip. Don't begin a long trip late in the day when you may run out of daylight, particularly those that have extensive forest distances. Save this time of day for short, local, exploratory trips.

Courtesy

Unfortunately, conflicts have developed in some parts of the country between mountain bike riders and other outdoor recreationists such as hikers and horse riders. Happily, this is not a problem in Vermont and hopefully will not become one. Using common sense and following a few rules of courtesy will help to ensure that no problem develops.

Respect the property of others. Don't ride on land that is posted without permission. Many landowners post land for a specific reason, such as to keep out hunters or motorized vehicles, and won't object to your quiet bicycle. Don't chase farm animals with a bike, and don't feed them. Horses and cows you see along the way might be worth hundreds, even thousands of dollars. A leg injury might be life-threatening to such large animals, as might eating certain kinds of vegetation that is poisonous.

Don't build fires, and don't litter. Carry out what you carry in.

Yield to others, and pass with care. This is particularly true when you encounter horses. Pull to the side, stop, and let the horse and rider pass. When approaching from behind, keep well back until the rider knows you are there. Ask in advance if it is safe to pass.

Information on Vermont

Vermont Atlas and Gazetteer, Delorme Publishing, P.O. Box 298, Freeport, Maine 04032.

Vermont Road Atlas and Guide, Northern Cartographic Inc., 10 W. Canal Street, Winooski, Vermont 05404

For general information about vacationing in Vermont:

Vermont: An Explorer's Guide by Christina Tree and Peter Jennison, Countryman Press, 1988.

Vermont Travel Division, 134 State Street, Montpelier, Vermont 05602 (802-828-3236).

For information on specific activities, attractions, and events:
Vermont Chamber of Commerce, Box 37, Montpelier, Vermont 05602 (802-223-3443).

For information on specific activities, attractions, and events, plus to make lodging reservations (no charge for the service):
Vermont Travel Information Service, Pond Village, Brookfield, Vermont 05036 (802-276-3120).

Information on Bicycling

National Bicycling Organizations

Bikecentennial, Inc., P.O. Box 8308, Missoula, MT 59807 (406-721-1776). A national service organization for recreational bicyclists that is member supported. They offer an extensive collection of cycling pamphlets and paraphernalia, as well as road tour maps of the country and a magazine published ten times a year. While concentration has been primarily on road touring in the past, they are beginning to include mountain bikes as part of their focus. Dues are $22 annually.

League of American Wheelmen (*Bicycle USA* magazine), Suite 209, 6707 Whitestone Road, Baltimore, MD 21207 (301-944-3399). Another national membership organization with a broader focus, emphasizing cycle touring, bicycle advocacy, and club cycling. Dues are $22 annually and include a subscription to the association's magazine, published nine times a year.

National Off-Road Bicycle Association (NORBA), 1750 East Boulder Street, Colorado Springs, CO 80909 (719-578-4717). An organization that promotes safe riding and the responsible use of public resources, as well as pursuing an interest in mountain bike racing. Annual dues of $18 include a subscription to its newsletter.

Publications

Bicycling Magazine, 33 E. Minor Street, Emmaus, PA 18049 (215-967-5171). Published by Rodale Press nine times a year, this magazine has a national circulation of over two million and has a broad editorial focus that includes racing and touring for both road and mountain bikes, as well as a commitment to fitness and training.

Fat Tire Flyer, P.O. Box 757, Fairfax, CA 94930 (415-457-7016). A bi-monthly magazine devoted to mountain bicycling.

All-Terrain Bikes, Rodale Press, Emmaus, PA, 1985.

The Complete Book of All-Terrain Bicycles by Eugene Sloan, Simon and Schuster, Inc., 1985.

Rides Rated By Difficulty

No.	Route	Rating	Miles
16.	North Danville	Easy	7.1
6.	Woodstock	Easy	8.9
3.	Putney	Easy	9.8
24.	South Hero	Easy	15.0
21.	Ferdinand	Easy/Moderate	15.6
14.	Groton	Easy/Moderate	12 or 19.4
22.	Richmond	Moderate	11.4
4.	Grafton	Moderate	14.1
1.	Bennington	Moderate	14.2
9.	Pittsfield	Moderate	15.0
2.	Arlington	Moderate	17.2
8.	Bethel	Moderate	18.4
15.	Kent Corners	Moderate	18.4
25.	Grand Isle	Moderate	18.8
5.	Wallingford	Mod./Strenuous	20.3
7.	Norwich	Mod./Strenuous	21.0
10.	Ripton	Mod./Strenuous	14.9 or 29.8
19.	Orleans	Strenuous	26.1
23.	Cambridge	Strenuous	24.7
12.	Braintree Hill	Strenuous	23.0
18.	Greensboro	Strenuous	26.7
13.	Graniteville	Strenuous	31.7
20.	Lake Willoughby	Strenuous	24.7
11.	Braintree Gap	Strenuous	26.0
17.	Victory	Strenuous	27.2

A quiet lane invites further exploration.

Southern Vermont

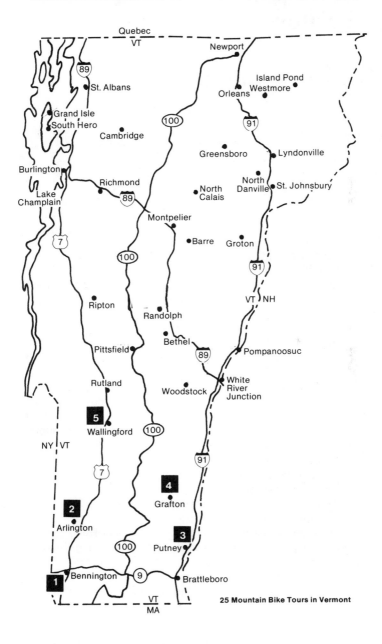

Quebec
VT

Newport

89

St. Albans

Island Pond
Orleans Westmore

Grand Isle
South Hero

100

Cambridge

91

Greensboro Lyndonville

Burlington

Richmond
89

North Calais

North
Danville St. Johnsbury

Lake
Champlain

Montpelier

7

Barre Groton

100

91

Ripton

VT NH

Randolph

100

Bethel

Pittsfield

89

Pompanoosuc

Rutland

Woodstock

White
River
Junction

5
Wallingford

100

NY VT

7

4
Grafton

91

2
Arlington

3
Putney

100

1 Bennington

9

Brattleboro

25 Mountain Bike Tours in Vermont

VT
MA

Bennington

Distance: 14.2 miles
Difficulty: Moderate
Riding surface: Primarily gravel, with some pavement
Towns included: Bennington, Pownal
Maps: USGS 7.5' Bennington, Pownal, North Pownal

First settled by six families who arrived in 1761, Bennington is Vermont's third largest city. Old Bennington, the area originally settled and where this trip begins and ends, is distinct from Bennington proper. This area is relatively flat, with the exception of 2,340-foot Mount Anthony, which looms in the southwest corner of town and around the flank of which this route winds in a counterclockwise direction.

August 16 is Bennington Battle Day, a state holiday in Vermont commemorating what some historians feel was the battle that turned the tide of the American Revolution. The battle was actually fought outside of Bennington in what is now New York. On that date in 1777, a ragtag band of two thousand mostly untrained Vermont woodsmen and farmers soundly defeated a well-equipped and trained complement of General Burgoyne's army, which was enroute to Bennington to appropriate American supplies located there. This defeat foiled Burgoyne's strategy to cut New England off from the rest of the colonies. It also played a major role in the surrender of his entire command of eight thousand troops less than two months later.

There is a lot to see and do around Bennington, and one of the more popular attractions is the Bennington Museum from which this trip begins. The museum has a large collection of decorative arts, furniture, and paintings, as well as historical artifacts from Vermont and New England. It has an important collection of American glass and the largest public collection of works by the American folk artist, Grandma Moses. It even has The Wasp, a 1925 luxury touring car designed and built with high-quality components by Karl Martin in Bennington. The Chamber of Commerce Information Building next to the deer park has an excellent assortment of information about the area, including a self-guided walking tour that can be covered by bike as well.

0.0 Begin at the Bennington Museum, located on VT 9 west of Bennington Village. Leaving the parking lot, turn LEFT onto VT 9 and begin to climb a hill. Continue straight past a cemetery on your left and the Monument Elementary School on your right.

0.4 Continue on VT 9 as it bends to the right next to the Walloomsac Inn. This is the heart of Old Bennington. The Walloomsac Inn was started in 1766 and is the oldest inn in Vermont. Across the way is the Old First Church, built in 1808 and considered one of the most beautiful in the state. This part of town also has more than eighty residences built in the Georgian and federal styles between 1770 and 1830.

0.8 Pass on your left the Camelot Village and Antique Center.

1.2 At the top of this rise, you can see the Bennington Airport to your right about a half mile away.

1.8 Turn LEFT onto the Mount Anthony Road. Directly across VT 9 at this road is the Fairdale Farms dairy. Closer to the road are an antique shop and an interesting silo with an outside surface of ceramic tile.

2.2 The road turns to dirt.

3.4 From here there are excellent views on your right.

The homesteads that sprang up around the foot of Mount Anthony and elsewhere in Vermont during the late 1700s produced potash as a sideline to farming, just as many of today's dairy farmers produce maple syrup or extra hay for needed cash.

There was a strong international market for potash. It was an essential ingredient for soap, and soaps were used in the manufacture of woolen cloth since cleansing the wool was required at several different stages. Much of the clothing worn in the world at that time was wool. A seventeenth-century English law even required that all corpses be buried in a wool shroud.

Since it was made from wood ashes, potash was a natural by-product of clearing land. The trees were cut down, cut into manageable pieces, and then burned. The ashes were soaked in large kettles of water to make lye, and finally the water was boiled off, leaving the black, solid potash. About five tons of wood, equal to three or four cords or one huge elm or maple, would make forty pounds of potash. The potash could then be easily transported by pack horse to market, where the quantity carried on a couple of

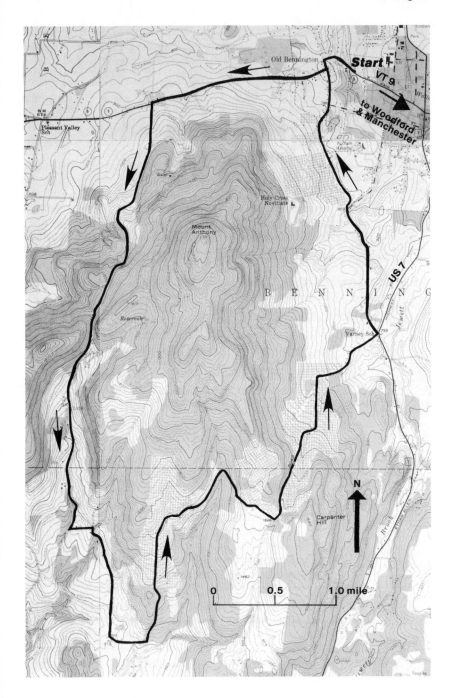

animals might fetch fifty dollars, a huge sum of money for those days.

In 1791 alone, two thousand tons of potash with a market value of nearly a million dollars were exported from Vermont, an amount that required the processing of nearly a half million cords of wood.

4.0 With much of the climbing behind you, the road begins to descend.

4.2 Pass on your left a horse farm with a red barn.

4.6 Pass on your right another residence with a red barn.

4.8 Pass an interesting octagonal camp on your right, and note the fine views to the south down the valley.

5.7 Turn LEFT.

5.9 Pass between a juxtaposition of two very different landscaping themes. On your right is a fine old Victorian residence painted yellow. Across the road to your left is a much smaller and plainer residence, with a permanent flock of plastic pink flamingoes on the front lawn.

6.1 There are excellent views to the west in this part of the trip, and the road ahead is narrow and lined with aged maples. It is apparent that over the years the highway crews that maintain the road have preferred to let the road narrow at this point rather than to disturb the trees that are close to it on either side.

6.8 Stay on the road as it curves to the left, past a couple of residences and a collection of heavy equipment on the right. Climb a short rise, and at the top be rewarded with excellent views in every direction.

7.0 Turn LEFT onto a much rougher road, and begin a gradual ascent.

7.7 You have now emerged from the forest and are passing between large fields on either side. As you near the top, there are marvelous views behind you to the south.

8.1 Turn RIGHT onto the well-maintained road, passing on your left a residence set back several hundred feet from the road.

8.9 Pass on your left a residence displaying a "Bee Hive" sign in front, and begin another climb of about a half mile. At the top of the hill is the beginning of a huge apple orchard, planted to new trees on your left and with mature trees on your right. The views are superb.

9.5 Turn LEFT.

10.1 The road becomes paved, and there are excellent views to the north; the Bennington Monument sits off to the left.

The Bennington Battle Monument is the tallest structure in Vermont and was completed in 1891, after four years of construction. It is 306-feet tall and made from blue-grey magnesian limestone that was quarried in Hudson Falls, New York. A bronze and gilt star at the top has points that are each eighteen inches long; it serves as a lightning rod for the structure. The visitor observation area is reached by an elevator that was added after the original construction.

A dramatic view to the south toward Massachusetts is the reward for those who reach the summit of this Bennington hill.

11.5   At this intersection with US 7, turn sharply LEFT away from US 7 and onto the adjacent paved road. Begin a brief but abrupt climb, with a more gradual climb beyond.

12.2   Pass the Hull House of Blue Hill on your right.

12.4   Continue STRAIGHT past Meadowbrook Drive on your right.

12.6   Turn LEFT following the directional sign to the hospital.

12.9   Pass the entrance road to the Southwest Medical Center Hospital on your right.

13.5   Pass Elm Street on your right.

13.8   Turn right onto VT 9 East, passing the front of the Walloomsac Inn on your left.

14.2   You have reached the Bennington Museum from which the trip began.

Accommodations
Greenwood Lodge and Tentsites, VT 9, Woodford, VT 05201 (802–442–2547). Located on 120 acres in an alpine meadow setting, this is a rustic lodge/hostel with two dorms, five private rooms, and twenty wooded tent sites. There are three small ponds for fishing, boating, and swimming. Dining is available for lodge guests only.

The South Shire Inn, 124 Elm Street, Bennington, VT 05201 (802–447–3839). This attractive Victorian mansion was built around the turn of the century in the heart of what is now historic Bennington and features antique furnishings, fireplace guestrooms, and canopy beds.

The Walloomsac Inn, Monument Avenue, Bennington, VT 05201 (802–442–4865). Little changed in two hundred years, this is Vermont's oldest inn and a unique lodging opportunity.

Bakers At Bennington, VT 7A, Bennington, VT 05201 (802–442–5619). Six guest rooms with shared baths in an 1859 country home. Mountain views; breakfast is included.

Camping
Woodford State Park, Bennington, VT 05201. Picnic tables and fireplaces, fishing, rental boats and canoes, hiking, nature trails, tent and trailer sites, lean-tos, and hot showers.

Bicycle Service
Battenkill Sports, Intersection of US 7 and VT 11–30, Manchester, VT (802–362–2734).

Cross Country Bicycle, P.O. Box 836, Route 100 N., Wilmington, VT (802–464–0432).

Up and Downhill, Inc., 160 Ben Mont Avenue, Bennington, VT (802–442–8664).

Arlington

Distance: 17.2 miles
Difficulty: Moderate
Riding surface: Primarily gravel, with some pavement
Towns included: Arlington, Sandgate, Sunderland
Maps: USGS 7.5' Arlington, West Rupert, Sunderland

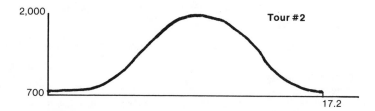

Arlington was first settled in 1763, and the names of many of the state's early prominent citizens are tied to the area, including Revolutionary War hero Ethan Allen and the state's first governor, Thomas Chittenden.

From 1939 to 1943, artist Norman Rockwell lived in Arlington where he painted many of the 321 *Saturday Evening Post* covers for which he is famous. Using over two hundred Arlington townspeople as models, Rockwell worked on several paintings at a time. Each took between two and three weeks to complete, although the depiction of Lindbergh's successful trans-Atlantic flight was done in a single day to meet the deadline. Norman Rockwell worked primarily in oil, although he sometimes used watercolors, charcoal, or pen. During his Arlington years, he used photography as an aid to capture the scenes he would paint, since the busy residents whose everyday lives he immortalized had neither the time, training, nor inclination to act as models. The artist died in 1978 at the age of eighty-four.

The Arlington Gallery, located in an historic 1875 church, was established in 1983 to display Norman Rockwell's work and to emphasize the important role the residents of the small town of Arlington played during some of Rockwell's most productive painting years. The gallery even employs a number of former models as guides.

Dorothy Canfield Fisher, author of fifty popular books, lived for many years in Arlington. The brick home of her family, who were among the earliest settlers of this town, is located across the street from this trip's starting point.

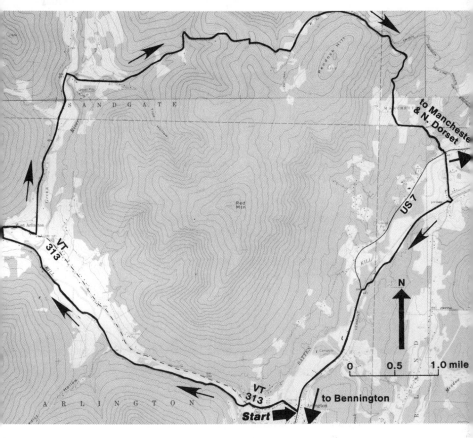

Elsewhere in town are the Canfield Pines, a forty-acre grove of some of the largest old white pines in the state. Some are nearly three feet in diameter and more than one hundred feet tall.

Mountain bikes can be rented north of Arlington in Manchester at the Battenkill Bicycle Shop, located at the intersection of US 7 and VT 11-30. Call ahead at 802–362–2734.

0.0 Begin on the drive in front of the St. James Episcopal Church. The church and the adjacent graveyard will be on your left, and the attractive brick building (circa 1829) that houses the Arlington Community Building and Canfield Library will be across VT 7 on your right. Proceed ahead a couple hundred feet and turn LEFT onto VT 313, which signs indicate will lead you to Sandgate and Cambridge.

The graveyard next to the church is one of the oldest in the state, and many of the old headstones have intriguing inscriptions. Mary Brownson, first wife of Ethan Allen, is buried here.

0.7 Turn LEFT onto River Road, passing on your right the Battenkill Canoe

Rentals headquarters. Cross the bridge just ahead, and turn RIGHT onto the dirt road.

> Battenkill Canoe Rentals offers a variety of services to those wishing to enjoy the Battenkill in a more intimate way. Supplying all the equipment you need for a trip lasting from two hours to two days, Battenkill Canoe Rentals will drop you off at the beginning of a river trip and pick you up at the end. If you prefer, they will arrange an overnight stay at selected country inns. In addition, their shop sells fine quality canoes, clothing, camping gear, and paddling accessories. For more information, they can be reached at 802–375–9559.

0.9 Bear RIGHT, and continue on this road as it follows the Battenkill River. Vermont is a state blessed with a multitude of streams that offer excellent trout fishing, but the Battenkill is legendary. Considered one of the best trout streams in the country, the Battenkill harbors skittish brook trout and big, wary brown trout that will reject the best efforts of even the most skilled fly fishermen. The name Battenkill is Dutch in origin, batten meaning "luxurious living" and kill translating to "river."

1.7 Pass on your left the Four Winds Country Inn Bed & Breakfast.

2.5 Continue STRAIGHT past the Benedict Hollow Road on your left.

2.9 Continue STRAIGHT past an interesting wooden framed bridge on your right, and climb a short rise up and away from the river.

4.4 Turn RIGHT onto Covered Bridge Road, and pass on your left the Battenkill Grange and Methodist Church, built in 1804. Pass through the covered bridge across the river.

> Built in 1852, spanning eighty feet, and built with a Town lattice structure, this bridge has provided service for more than 135 years. The Town lattice structure takes its name from Ithiel Town, a Connecticut man who patented the design in 1820 and then traveled throughout this country and Europe to sell his patents. The cross-hatched lattice design pattern is easily recognizable and was used on hundreds of bridges throughout the country. The individual lattice sections were usually pegged with wooden "trunnels."

4.5 Turn RIGHT onto VT 313 after passing through the covered bridge.

4.9 Turn LEFT onto the Sandgate Road, and enjoy an excellent view to the north up the valley toward Mount Equinox. There is a climb here for about a half mile. Below the road to the right is the Green River, one of many mountain streams that feed the Battenkill.

6.5 Pass the Swearing Hill Farm.

An unusual traffic sign in Arlington cautions about a different kind of traffic.

6.8   Turn RIGHT onto the Southeast Corner Road, cross the bridge over the Green River, and begin a short but steep climb.

6.9   Continue STRAIGHT past a road on the left. For the next 2 1/2 miles, the trip climbs along the northern slope of Red Mountain before leveling off and descending the other side.

8.4   Keep to the LEFT, passing a private road on your right.

8.5   Follow the road as it bends sharply to the right and climbs steeply. At the same time, the surface of the road deteriorates as it becomes less of a gravel road and more of a forest trail.

9.6   The road flattens out before beginning to drop.

10.5 The trail emerges from the forest into a clearing, with a large red vehicle maintenance building on the right. Just ahead you come to a "No Trespassing" sign that proclaims the area ahead to be a state game refuge, although it is apparently privately operated.

   Stay on the trail you have been traveling as it continues to the RIGHT of the sign, and be ready for the thunderous winged departure of ruffed grouse that frequent the edge of this road.

11.1 Pass between a building on your left and a collapsed camp on your right.

11.6 Just as the road begins a particularly steep plunge, you will catch sight of a paved road that winds up the mountain to your left.

   This road to the left is the Sky Line Drive, a five-mile toll road to the summit of Equinox Mountain. Equinox is the tallest peak of the Taconic Range at 3,816 and offers splendid views of the winding Battenkill and surrounding area. It's also the site of the largest wind turbine farm in the Northeast, the propellers of which can be seen from the valley below. This is a worthwhile side trip by automobile.

12.6 The trail emerges from the forest, with a new saltbox-style residence on the right overlooking extensive fields where Hereford beef cattle graze. Here the trail becomes a well-maintained road and continues the descent.

13.5 Continue STRAIGHT across VT 7A, and cross the Battenkill. Use caution crossing the highway, for this road is heavily traveled. Although you could turn right onto VT 7A at this junction and return directly to the starting point, you would have to contend with a significant volume of traffic. After crossing the river, continue STRAIGHT, over a high railroad bridge.

14.1 Turn RIGHT at this intersection, and then turn RIGHT again sharply onto a dirt road that dips down slightly. You'll pass the Sunderland Town Highway Garage on your right as you make the turn.

This stretch of the road provides a good view to the west of the mountainous terrain that you traveled in the middle portion of this trip.

15.6 Turn LEFT onto VT 7 and head back to the starting point, passing in succession on your right The Edgewood Restaurant, The Cheese House, The Candlelight Motel, and The Sugar Shack.

16.8 Pass on your right the Arlington Recreation Field.

17.2 You have arrived back at the Episcopal Church from which you began the trip.

Accommodations

The Arlington Inn, VT 7A, Arlington, VT 05250 (802-375-2839).
    One of the state's finest Greek revival mansions, with nicely restored rooms furnished with antiques. Candlelight dinners, Sunday brunch, tennis.
The Sycamore Inn, VT 7A, Box 2485, Arlington, VT 05250 (802-362-2284).
    Home-style atmosphere in a two hundred-year-old inn. The inn's property fronts the Battenkill for fishing or swimming; full breakfast included.
The Inn on Covered Bridge Green, RD 1, Box 3550, West Arlington, VT 05250 (802-375-9489).
    Built around 1792 and once owned by Norman Rockwell, this colonial farmhouse offers the comforts and elegance of the past. Breakfast included; fireside refreshments, games, library, tennis, close to the Battenkill.
The Evergreen Inn, Sandgate Road, Box 2480, Arlington, VT 05250 (802-375-2272).
    Casual, relaxed atmosphere, beautiful scenery, family owned and operated for fifty years. Full breakfast and dinner included, home cooking and baking.
The Hill Farm Inn, RR2, Box 2015, Arlington, VT 05250 (802-375-2269).
    On the Battenkill, this quiet and comfortable country inn features a farm setting and great mountain views. Delicious country cooking with home-grown vegetables, home-baked breads, and desserts. This 1790 guest house is situated on fifty acres of land bordering the Battenkill.

Camping

Camping on the Battenkill, VT 7A, Arlington, VT 05250.
    Picnic tables and fireplaces, fishing, swimming, and tubing in the Battenkill, hiking, 103 sites (about half wooded), hot showers. Reservations recommended.
Emerald Lake State Park, North Dorset, VT 05251.
    Picnic tables and fireplaces, fishing, rental boats and canoes, hiking, nature trails, tent and trailer sites, and hot showers.

Bicycle Service

Battenkill Sports, Intersection of US 7 and VT 11-30, Manchester, VT (802-362-2734).
Cross Country Bicycle, P.O. Box 836, Route 100 N., Wilmington, VT (802-464-0432).
Up and Downhill, Inc., 160 Ben Mont Avenue, Bennington, VT (802-442-8664).

Putney

Distance: 9.8 miles
Difficulty: Easy
Riding surface: Gravel, pavement
Towns included: Putney, Westminster
Maps: USGS 15' Bellows Falls, Keene (NH)

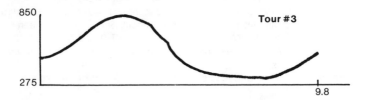

Putney is a community rich in history and has been a cultural refuge for artists, writers, and craftspeople for many years. It is the home of The Putney School, a college prep school founded more than fifty years ago with the philosophy that students will cultivate a sense of self-sufficiency by helping raise their own food. Putney is also home to Landmark College, a school that specializes in providing college educations for dyslexic students.

Elsewhere in town can be found the Green Mountain Spinnery, a relatively new business where Vermont fleeces are made into yarn, The Putney Nursery, with a magnificent selection of wildflowers, and Basketville, with its huge inventory of basketry.

A part of Putney's legacy that the Chamber of Commerce would probably like to forget but that is inevitably included with every account of the town is the story of John Noyes. Noyes founded a religious colony in Putney in 1838. The ideas were progressive: In addition to believing that all work was dignified and that women had the same rights as men, Noyes and his followers believed that total sharing among members was necessary to reach the state of perfection required by God, a sharing that included not only cattle, corn, and chores, but also child care and even spouses. In his own words from a letter published at the time, "In a holy community there is no more reason why sexual intercourse should be restrained by law, than why eating or drinking should be — and there is as little occasion for shame in one case as in the other."

This last tenet was more than his conservative Putney neighbors

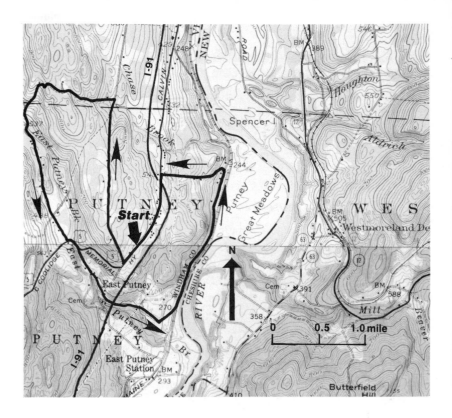

could tolerate: Noyes was arrested in 1847. While released on bond for his trial appearance, Noyes seized what may have been his final opportunity at freedom and fled to Oneida, New York. He was later joined by many of his followers to found the Oneida Community and eventually to produce Oneida Silver. To placate his neighbors in his new town, Noyes agreed to defer to public sentiment and discontinue the practice of what he called "complex marriage."

0.0 Begin with Harlow's Sugar House on your left. Head south on US 5 and prepare to take the first road on your right just ahead.

Harlow's Sugar House is one of the largest agricultural tourist attractions in southeastern Vermont. Pick-your-own strawberries are sold here during the last week of June and first weeks of July, blueberries are sold in August, apples in September and October (Putney's large apple industry makes up ten percent of the state's crop), and maple syrup, year-round. There is an educational exhibit and movie of maple sugaring, and you can even enjoy a sleigh ride during the sugaring season (although you won't be riding your bike at that time of year).

0.1 Turn RIGHT onto Pine Banks Road and begin a brief climb.

1.9 Turn LEFT onto Quarry Road and climb. A sign here warns traffic that the road ahead is narrow and winding.

2.8 The road drops sharply around a hairpin curve and passes two residences.
> There is an extremely interesting landscape around these buildings. Opening to a distant view of the southwest, the surrounding fields are adorned with many large metal sculptures, each with a distinctive and attractive geometric shape and each probably weighing several hundred pounds.

3.1 Turn LEFT at the intersection.

3.4 Cross a wooden bridge and turn LEFT.

3.5 Pass the Brookside Camping Ground on the right, with East Putney Brook on the left.
> There apparently are some interesting falls and potholes somewhere on this brook, but I don't know where they are. You might inquire at the campground if you wish to make an interesting side trip.

4.4 Continue STRAIGHT on the Putney Brook Road at this four-way intersection.

4.8 Turn LEFT onto paved US 5, then turn RIGHT onto East Putney Falls Road, the first road on the right that you encounter.

5.4 Pass on your left the Spaulding Hill Road, and just beyond, pass a road on the right.

5.5 Pass Pierce's Hall on the left.
> Built in 1831, this building was originally the Methodist Church. After the congregation outgrew the building, it was used for a different kind of flock: Sheep were sheltered beneath it, while corn was stored on the first floor. It eventually became the headquarters for the East Putney Community Club, an organization established to promote the moral, intellectual, and social life of its members.

5.7 Pass under the I-91 overpass.

6.4 Turn LEFT onto the River Road. Railway tracks parallel the road on your right, as does the Connecticut River.
> Here the river is deep and flows slowly, part of a thirty-one-mile unobstructed stretch between the dams at Vernon to the south and at Bellows Falls to the north. This is a popular part of the river for canoeing as well as power boating. The fishing is good in the Connecticut River as it flows by Vermont, and three of the state's record fish have been caught in the river — a nine-pound bass, a

twelve-pound walleyed pike, and a seventeen-pound tiger muskie pike. There are also rich concentrations of waterfowl on this stretch of the river.

Ferries plied the river for many of the early years of settlement, but bridges gradually took their place. One such bridge located near this stretch was the scene of a tragic accident in 1818. A traveling circus was on its way to town, causing much excitement and bringing many of the local residents to the river to await its arrival. An initial survey of the bridge by circus personnel deemed it safe to cross, but the elephant balked — perhaps warned by the sixth sense that some animals seem to possess. Not to be deterred from their plan, the circus staff proceeded to force the reluctant pachyderm across the bridge against its will. When it was nearly to the opposite side, the floor of the bridge collapsed with a splintering crash under the unaccustomed weight. The unfortunate elephant clutched at a beam with its trunk, hung on for a brief moment, and then plunged with shrieks of terror onto the rocks below before the horrified crowd. The beast's back was broken, and it was destroyed. The skin was stuffed and was later displayed in a Boston museum for many years.

7.5 A road on the right passes through a cement tunnel under the train tracks.

Opposite that road is an historic site marker showing the location of the Putney Forts on the Great Meadows, site of the first settlement in Putney. The Great Meadows area along the river has long been prized for its fertile, easily cultivated soil, and even today it is planted to corn by local farmers.

Settlement here began with the building of a fort after the Cape Breton war ended in 1744. The area was still very much a frontier at that point, and hostile Indian activity was an ongoing threat. The first Indian attack made on the fort's personnel occurred on July 5, 1745, when William Phipps was accosted by two Indians while hoeing corn outside the fort. Phipps was forced into the nearby woods and left under the guard of one of the Indians. Phipps gained freedom by attacking the guard with his hoe, which for some reason he was allowed to keep, and then using the guard's rifle to shoot the second captor, who was just returning. He then ran for the fort but was killed by three more Indians that he encountered on the way. Indian harassment and attacks fatal to both the settlers and their livestock continued during the next two years, and the fort was finally abandoned as its inhabitants relocated to a safer territory. The Indians had thus won the first round.

The abandoned fort quickly turned into ruins, and the forest made steady progress toward reclaiming the area around it. Then, in 1755, a new fort was built. Stout walls of six-inch, hand hewn pine timbers standing seventeen-feet high formed a compound measuring 120 by 80 feet. Sixteen houses were built within the fortress, with the back wall of each formed by the main outside wall and the front of each house facing the center of the compound. Roofs of the houses sloped upwards toward the top of the wall. The main gate to the fort was located on the east wall facing the river, while a smaller gate opened to the south.

8.0   Turn LEFT onto the Old Fort Road, passing an attractive old brick house on the left and another equally attractive brick house just ahead to the right. A fairly steep climb of about a half mile begins here.

8.8   Turn LEFT onto US 5.

9.0   Cross the bridge over I-91.

9.3   Pass Santa's Land on the right, then the Igloo Pancake House on the right also.

9.8   You have arrived back at Harlow's Sugar House.

Accommodations
The Hickory Ridge House, RFD 3, Box 1410, Putney, VT 05346 (802–387–5709).
> A gracious 1808 brick Georgian home on a country road near the Connecticut River and two miles from Putney Village. Guest rooms with fireplaces and an elegant country breakfast including homemade jams and jellies, baked goods, and home-produced eggs, honey, and maple syrup.

Misty Meadows, RD 1, Box 458, Putney, VT 05346 (802–722–9517).
> Comfortable country rooms with fine views of the Connecticut River Valley. Full country breakfast, served on the patio or by the fire; many acres of woods and pasture to wander.

The Putney Inn, Depot Road, Putney, VT 05346 (802–387–5517).
> This red clapboard building is one of the oldest farmhouses in the area and was retrofitted as a lodging establishment in the 1960s. Public rooms in the original building, with additional motel units.

Camping
Townsend State Park, Newfane, VT 05345.
> Picnic tables and fireplaces, fishing in nearby streams, hiking, tent and trailer sites, lean-tos, and hot showers.

Jamaica State Park, Jamaica, VT 05343.
> Picnic tables and fireplaces, fishing in nearby streams, hiking, tent and trailer sites, lean-tos, and hot showers.

Bicycle Service
Brattleboro Bike Shop, 178 Main Street, Brattleboro, VT (802–254–8644).
Specialized Sports, Putney Road, Brattleboro, VT (802–257–1017).
West Hill Shop, Depot Road, Putney, VT (802–387–5718).

Grafton

Distance: 14.1 miles
Difficulty: Moderate
Riding surface: Gravel, with some pavement
Towns included: Grafton, Chester
Map: USGS 15' Saxton's River

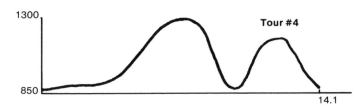

Grafton was originally called Thomlinson by those who settled it in the early 1780s. The name was changed to Grafton after the early residents deemed it inappropriate that their town should be named after an out-of-state landowner who had never set foot in it. The right to select the new name was auctioned off for five dollars and a jug of rum, and the high bidder chose the name of his hometown: Grafton, Massachusetts.

Although it is hard to imagine today, by the 1950s the fortunes of Grafton had declined to such a state that many of the local properties had taken on an untidy, unkempt appearance. This trend was reversed, however, through renovations and preservations sponsored by The Windham Foundation. This not-for-profit organization was established in 1963 with funds bequeathed by Mrs. Rodney Fiske of New York City, who had owned a vacation home in Grafton. It is the largest foundation in the state and pursues three purposes: to restore buildings and economic vitality to the village of Grafton, to provide financial support for education and private charities, and to develop projects that benefit the general welfare of Vermont and Vermonters.

The foundation has purchased and renovated more than twenty buildings over the last twenty years, including several private houses, a dairy farm, the village store, and a blacksmith. It has also acquired a thousand acres of surrounding land that is managed for wildlife preservation, hiking, and cross-country skiing. It created the Grafton Cheese Company, where cheese is still made largely by hand, to stimulate the local economy. Also outstanding among the foundation's many notable

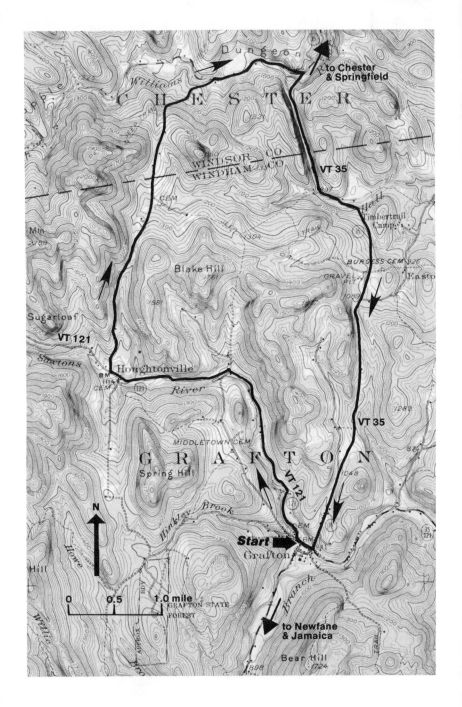

projects has been the restoration of the Old Tavern, a popular vacation spot for many famous people during the nineteenth century including Rudyard Kipling, Teddy Roosevelt, Woodrow Wilson, and Henry David Thoreau. By the early 1900s, however, the inn had begun to lose its glory. Because it was unheated, it was closed every winter, and it changed hands a number of times. With each new owner came modifications to the interior, creating a hodgepodge of patchwork remodeling and flimsy paneling. Through the efforts of the Windham Foundation, the inn has now been completely remodeled inside to include central heating, a sprinkler system, an elevator, and private baths in each room. All renovation work has been done with strict attention to authenticity and craftsmanship, and the many antique furnishings were selected to match the original decor.

Other foundation projects include exhibits, displays, public forums, scholarship programs, and a multitude of charitable contributions to worthy Vermont organizations. The success of the foundation is witnessed by the thousands of tourists who visit Grafton every year to enjoy the traditional flavor and beauty of the village.

0.0 Begin with the Grafton Post Office on your right. Across the street, just ahead and on your left, is the restored Old Tavern At Grafton, circa 1801.

0.1 Turn RIGHT, following the sign for VT 121 West.

0.2 The pavement ends, and the Saxtons River parallels the road.

The distinctive plant growing along the side of the stream is bamboo, and for the next couple of miles, this stand continues to form one of the largest concentrations to be found in Vermont. A member of the buckwheat family and originally cultivated as food, bamboo came to Vermont from Japan via Belgium. In the last century, it was planted extensively and can be found near many old cellar holes and other locations that are not regularly mowed. Although some consider its young shoots quite edible, similar to asparagus when chilled and dressed as a salad, most landowners consider bamboo a nuisance, finding it nearly impossible to eradicate.

1.4 Pass the Grafton Village Apple Company and Country Store where you can buy apples, cider, cheese, and other products.

2.2 Continue on VT 121, marked here by directional arrows pointing to the left.

2.8 Pavement begins again.

3.3 Continue on this road as it bends to the right and approaches a cluster of homes in Houghtonville, a settlement established at about the same time as Grafton Village.

3.6 Turn RIGHT onto a dirt road with a large handsome brick house on the right, and prepare for a climb.

  This road is the old stagecoach route to Chester and has been in use for more than 150 years. The brick house on the corner is the Oliver Davis House, built in the early nineteenth century and owned by Oliver Davis, an early settler who came to town in 1788. Mr. Davis was married three times. His first wife died of measles only thirty days after the marriage; his other two marriages, however, produced in combination seventeen children.

  Large families were common in town. Another Davis family had sixteen children, and the Amsdens had seventeen. But the productivity record was held by Mr. and Mrs. Emery who had twenty-one children. Local history records that Sunday worshippers dreaded the arrival of the Emerys at church on cold winter days, since the door had to remain open so long while they all filed in.

4.1 The top of the climb is reached, and the road is lined on the right with aged maples, some of which probably witnessed the old stagecoaches passing by. Beyond the maples to the right, the land drops away into a deep ravine, a precipitous drop that possibly made faint-hearted coach passengers uneasy.

4.4 Pass on the left an interesting modern residence, with another one just past it on the left.

  Buildings such as these employ the latest in construction methods, materials, and household conveniences. The early residents of Grafton, however, were happy with a lot less. One of the things a husband could do to make his wife happy was to devise a way to duct water directly into the house from a spring above. Wood tubing was sometimes used, but in Grafton there was another usable substance that didn't leave a taste in the water as wood does — soapstone. Soapstone was readily available in town, and quarrying it was Grafton's chief industry for fifty years. Twenty men were employed to quarry the four hundred tons extracted annually. Soapstone can be easily cut and could be made into water pipes with relative ease. Cut into long, thin, rectangular shapes and drilled lengthwise through the middle, lengths of two to three feet were joined together with nipples to form a continuous line. If you could afford to buy it ready-made at the store, the price was a dollar per rod (sixteen feet). Soapstone water lines are still uncovered occasionally during excavation.

5.1 The land on either side opens up into meadows, and birches mingle with the maples along the road to make an attractive lane.

5.6 Bear LEFT at this intersection, where a sign points to the right and the Old Cobb Cemetery.

This cemetery is only a short distance. Should you wish to visit it, remember to adjust your odometer readings accordingly.

Tombstone epitaphs strive to capture the essence of a person's life in just a line or two. A few words, though, would not suffice to summarize the sadness endured by Fannie Taylor, a Grafton resident in the mid-1800s who married Horace Taylor and had four sons and a daughter. In 1856 son Harry was killed in an explosion at the powder factory where he worked. A year later, the Taylors' horses spooked while they were driving to church, and in the accident that ensued, Mrs. Taylor broke both wrists and her husband was killed. The next tragedy occurred in 1860 when a second son was killed in Civil War action. The third son was reported missing in action shortly afterward but was subsequently released as a prisoner of war. The fourth son was mentally retarded and lived at home with his mother. In 1861 the daughter married and moved to Missouri with her new husband. A short time later, the bride's new husband was struck by lightning and killed while he lay in bed next to her.

After her husband's accident, Fannie Taylor sold her farm to the town of Grafton for use as the town poor farm. This early form of social welfare ensured that the very poor would have food to eat and a roof over their heads. The town poor lived at the farm, and the able-bodied were expected to raise vegetables to eat, tend chickens for eggs, and so on. They could sell the surplus, and whatever additional support was required would be subsidized by the town.

Later, the poor farm concept was abandoned in favor of placement in private homes. Townspeople would "bid" on keeping a person for a year, and the low bidder would house and feed one of the impoverished in return for a subsidy paid for by the town. The poor were expected to assist in the sponsoring home by doing housework and farm chores.

Although the media in recent years has presented the plight of the homeless as a new phenomenon, communities like Grafton were addressing it more than one hundred years ago.

6.3 Pass on the left a barn labeled "Maple Hill Farm; Chester, Vermont" and prepare for the road to begin a steep descent.

7.2 Turn RIGHT onto a paved road, with the Williams River South Branch flowing on the left.

8.3 Turn RIGHT onto paved VT 35 and begin a steep ascent of a half mile or so.

VT 35 is popular with bicycle tourists, and you are likely to encounter groups of them pedaling north toward you.

Many of the state's country lanes are shaded by maples dating to the last century.

10.0 Here begins another climb, and there is rolling ascent for nearly a mile and a half.

11.3 By this point, the climbing is mostly finished.

13.1 Pass on the right the sheep pastures and barn of the Windham Foundation Sheep Project.

The Windham Foundation's flock of two hundred ewes produces

one hundred lambs for market through the Yankee Shepherds Co-operative, and yarn from the flock is available in Grafton shops. In addition, the project is steadily reclaiming land, selectively replacing forest with productive pasture much as the original settlers did. Today, though, modern equipment and management practices make the job a lot easier.

13.9 Turn RIGHT onto VT 121 after a swooping descent into Grafton Village.

14.1 You have arrived back at the starting point.

Accommodations

The Stronghold Inn, HCR 40, Grafton, VT 05146 (802–843–2203).
> A bed & breakfast inn housed in an 1820 farmhouse and located a half mile from the village. Furnished with antiques and handmade quilts, complete breakfast, private bathrooms, antique shop on premises.

The Inn at Woodchuck Hill Farm, Middletown Road, Grafton, VT 05146 (802–843–2398).
> Two miles west of the village, this 1780s inn on a two hundred-acre estate can accommodate twenty guests, has a seventy-five-mile view of distant mountains, and offers hiking trails and a swimming pond on the property. Rates include a hearty continental breakfast, and an antique shop is run in the old barn.

The Old Tavern, Main Street, Grafton, VT 05146 (802–843–2231).
> See description above; formal early American setting, tennis courts, swimming pond with sandy bottom. Can accommodate one hundred guests, but make reservations well in advance.

The Hayes House, Bear Hill Road, Grafton, VT 05146 (802–843–2461).
> Comfortable old house on a quiet back street by a covered bridge, just a four-minute walk to the village. A big fireplace for cool evenings; breakfast included with homemade breads, jellies, and jams. Reasonable rates.

Camping

Jamaica State Park, Jamaica, VT 05343.
> Picnic tables and fireplaces, fishing in nearby streams, hiking, tent and trailer sites, lean-tos, and hot showers.

Townsend State Park, Newfane, VT 05345.
> Picnic tables and fireplaces, fishing in nearby streams, hiking, tent and trailer sites, lean-tos, and hot showers.

Bicycle Service

A.B. Carpenter, VT 103, Chester Depot, VT (802–875–2676).
Dave's Bicycle Shop, Union Street, Springfield, VT (802–885–5888).
Mountain Cycology, Lamere Square, P.O. Box 527, Ludlow VT (802–228–2722).

Wallingford

Distance: 20.3 miles
Difficulty: Moderate/Strenuous
Riding surface: Gravel, with some pavement
Towns included: Wallingford, Clarendon, Tinmouth
Maps: USGS 15' Wallingford; USGS 7.5' Rutland, West Rutland, Middletown
Springs

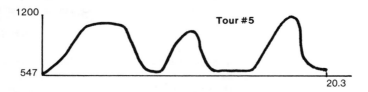

An unusually peaceful and attractive town divided in the middle by Otter Creek, Wallingford has a long heritage of upholding traditional Vermont values. Agriculture has long been a staple occupation in the area, and the village has supported a variety of small industry in the past.

In the early years of settlement before Vermont became an independent state, the ownership of land in Wallingford — as in much of settled Vermont at the time — was contested. New Yorkers and New Hampshirites each claimed it to be theirs, while many of the stubborn settlers had their own independence in mind. When farms were abandoned for a time during the Revolutionary War, squatters moved in and numerous confrontations occurred when the rightful owners returned after the war.

The first recorded death in Wallingford was a killing. A Tory sympathizer from Manchester was fleeing through town toward the safety of Castleton when local ruffians got word of his presence. They pursued him onto the hill west of town near where this tour begins, and when he in panic raised his rifle generally toward the crowd, they shot him dead. There is no record of anyone being tried for this crime, however. The first recorded public trial in town involved a town clerk, Stephen Arnold. His offense was neither embezzlement nor misuse of his office, as might be suspected, but "uttering extraordinary and offensive oathes." The case was excused when the circumstances became known during the trial. Arnold had been trying to pull a woodchuck from a crevice in a rock, with a thumb hooked in the rodent's mouth for a grip, when the 'chuck bit him and held on. Why he was trying to catch the woodchuck or what he

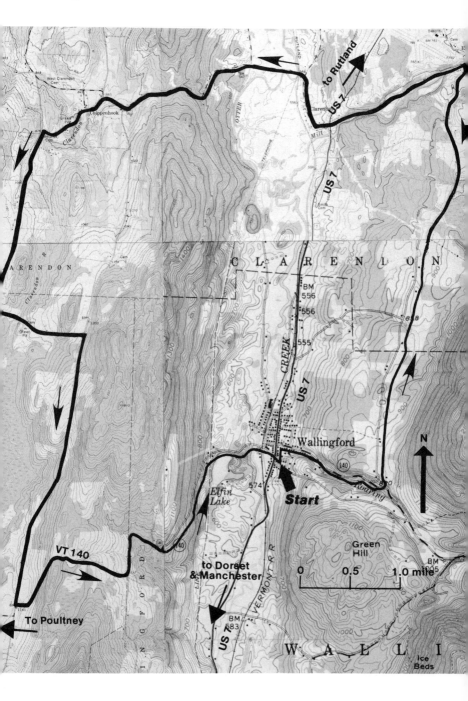

to Rutland

US 7

US 7

Chippenhook

OTTER

CLARENDON

BM
556

556

555

CREEK

US 7

858

N

Wallingford

140

Start

Elfin
Lake

574

VT 140

To Poultney

to Dorset
& Manchester

US 7

BM
583

Green
Hill

0   0.5   1.0 mile

BM
1005

W   A   L   L   I

Ice
Beds

intended to do with it are interesting questions whose answers have been lost to history.

The Old Stone Shop on Wallingford's Main Street is a Vermont landmark. Built in 1848 by Batchellors and Sons, the building's initial use was as a factory for manufacturing their famous pitchforks and other farm implements, a line they began in 1808. In 1902 they merged with the True Temper firm, which in addition to continuing the operation in town undertook a complete rebuilding of the Wallingford Inn, from the front porch of which Teddy Roosevelt delivered a campaign speech in 1912.

Wallingford's Main Street, widened considerably in 1937 to accommodate the highway, includes numerous other fine old buildings, many of which are good examples of the "third generation" of Vermont homes in many of the state's villages. The first generation consisted of log cabins built by the early settlers. Next were the single-story houses with a central chimney and a couple of rooms off the kitchen. Then in the early 1800s came the gracious and roomy homes such as these, with several rooms and from three to six fireplaces. Metal stoves for heating and cooking replaced fireplaces in such homes in the 1840s, and central heating with wood-fired, gravity hot air furnaces came in in the late 1800s.

Often the parlor was reserved as the "best room" where visitors were entertained, wakes conducted, and other formal affairs were held. Parlors were located on the north side of the house so that the carpets and other furnishings would not be faded by the sunlight. No indoor plumbing was available through much of the nineteenth century, but water for cooking and bathing was drawn into the house through a wooden conduit by an iron pump mounted next to the kitchen sink. Since most of the spring water was hard, softer rainwater was collected using eave troughs and stored in a cistern or rain barrel.

0.0 Start this trip in front of the Wallingford Block building, facing the stop light and with the building to your right. Begin by turning RIGHT immediately at the stop light onto VT 140. Pass the Wallingford House on your left and begin to climb.

0.1 Pass the Wallingford Town Hall on your left and continue to climb this winding, paved road with Roaring Brook cascading downhill to your right.

1.1 Turn LEFT onto East Street and climb one more rise that is abrupt but brief.

1.3 Turn LEFT at the top of the hill and follow the road as it bends sharply to the right.

Bear Mountain is the prominent hill on your right, with an elevation of 2,240 feet.

2.3 Pass the Bit O' Wind Farm, with the red barn on your right directly across the road from the white farmhouse.

2.8 Continue STRAIGHT past a road on your left, at the same time passing on your right the large horse pastures of The Salem Farm.

3.4 Pass the Spencer Brothers' Farm of registered Holsteins.

4.7 Continue STRAIGHT past a road on the left.

5.2 The area becomes more thickly settled as you enter the small village of East Clarendon.

5.6 Turn LEFT at the stop sign immediately after crossing the covered bridge, and begin a gradual downhill run for the next 1 1/2 miles.

To the left, the Mill River crashes over a series of ledges on its way to meet Otter Creek. Upstream from here is the Clarendon Gorge, a spectacular scene where the water spills through cliffs towering one hundred feet or more on each side. Just above the gorge, the Long Trail crosses the stream on a suspension bridge built in 1973. If you choose to make the short side trip to the gorge, remember to compensate for the additional distance on your odometer.

7.1 Proceed STRAIGHT across busy US 7 with great caution. This is a divided highway, with vehicles traveling in two lanes in both directions at fairly high rates of speed.

7.4 Pass on your left the Clarendon Town Office and, across the road on your right, the brick Clarendon Congregational Church.

7.7 Turn LEFT onto the Walker Mountain Road, passing on your right the Clarendon Auto Body Shop. Cross a set of railroad tracks, then ride over Otter Creek and continue STRAIGHT as the road passes between large corn fields on either side.

8.3 Continue STRAIGHT through this four-way intersection, and begin a mile-long climb up this paved road.

9.3 With the climb complete, the road levels off for a short distance before descending the other side.

10.0 Continue on paved road as it bends to the left, passing a dirt road on the right.

This is the settlement of Chippenhook, an old village settled before 1800. The Clarendon River flows through the valley and offers good trout fishing, and the old stone mill, built more than 150 years ago for grinding grist and pressing cider, is close to the road and under apparent renovation.

10.3 Turn LEFT, and at this point the pavement gives way to a gravel surface.

For the next couple of miles, the road dips up and down abruptly, creating a rollercoaster effect.

10.8 Turn LEFT.

11.3 Pass a red barn on your left bearing a sign for the Chippengym School of Gymnastics.

12.7 Turn LEFT.

12.9 Cross the Clarendon River once again.

13.6 Turn RIGHT onto Town Highway 7.

15.6 The road straightens out before you, and a good view down the valley to the south becomes available. Just downhill from this spot, you pass on your right a green barn with a rounded roof.

High on the hill to your left is a typical Vermont sugarhouse set in a well-manicured sugar bush. Many Vermont farmers and many non-farmers still devote three or four weeks during the spring "mud season" to making maple syrup, a hard, time-consuming activity that a lot of sugarmakers claim may not make good economic sense but that "gets in your blood." Most producers today no longer use buckets hung on individual trees but rather use plastic pipelines that enable the sap to flow under gravity right to the sugarhouse. There it is boiled so that water is removed from the sap, leaving only the concentrated syrup. Recent technological developments such as the reverse osmosis process mechanically reduce the water-to-sugar ratio before the actual boiling begins.

Four taps in a maple tree yield about forty gallons of sap, which when boiled down make one gallon of syrup. Originally, the sap was boiled beyond the syrup point to make sugar, which was more easily transported and widely in demand — hence the term "sugaring," which is still used exclusively to describe the process of making syrup.

Vermonters tap about two million maple trees annually to make about a half million gallons of syrup. Concern for the health of this traditional hillside industry has been raised by several consecutive years of poor production caused by a mix of climatic oddities. Long-term prospects are also a concern, for the state's trees — which may take from fifty to seventy-five years to mature — have been threatened by environmental stresses such as acid rain and roadside salt, as well as by insect pests such as the gypsy moth caterpillar and recently discovered pear thrips.

16.3 Turn LEFT onto VT 140 and begin a climb on paved surface.

16.8 Pass the back side of the sugar bush you viewed previously from the valley, with a good view of the valley below.

17.0 You have now reached the top of the hill and have before you an extended steep and winding descent on a paved surface into the valley. This road sometimes has a moderate amount of traffic and doesn't have pavement on the shoulder, so care should be exercised during the descent.

17.4 Pass on your left The Windswept Farm sign.

This section offers excellent views of the hills to the west, along which the Appalachian Trail passes, and to the northwest toward the major ski areas of Killington and Pico near the Mendon Mountain area.

Directly across the valley is the prominent White Rocks area, a conspicuous white pile of tumbled rocks that can be seen for miles around. The slide happened thousands of years ago, but the hard surface of the quartzite rock prevents vegetation from gaining a foothold. Winter snow penetrates deep into the slide, out of reach of the sun, creating "ice caves" that remain frozen to release cold drafts and a rivulet of ice water well into the summer. Local legend has it that a cave containing a rich lode of silver is located beneath the slide, but investigations including the use of explosives have failed to discover it.

Across the ridges above the slide passes the Long Trail. This particular section was opened in 1917, seven years after the Green Mountain Club was founded.

19.7 Pass on your RIGHT Elfin Lake, where ice was cut by the villagers before refrigeration became available in the 1920s, and a sign for the public beach on the eastern shore.

20.0 Cross Otter Creek once again.

20.1 Continue on VT 140 as it bends to the LEFT and then, in a couple hundred feet, toward the RIGHT.

20.3 You have reached the intersection in front of the Wallingford Block where the trip started.

Accommodations

The White Rocks Inn, R.R. 1, Box 297, US 7, Wallingford, VT 05773 (802-446-2077).

An elegantly furnished 1840s farmhouse and a spectacular barn, both on the National Register of Historic Places, offers beautiful antiques, canopy beds, and private baths in a relaxing, pastoral setting. Full breakfast included.

The Dunham House, 7 South Main Street, Wallingford, VT 05773 (802-446-2600).

Very attractive 1856 Victorian home, delicious home-cooked breakfast, carriage house with sauna, whirlpool, and exercise room.

The Wallingford Inn, US 7, Wallingford, VT 05773 (802–446–2849).

> This Victorian townhouse, owned by the family of True Temper Tool fame until 1969, features handsome woodwork, marble fireplaces, rooms with bath, and a continental breakfast.

The Green Mountain Guest House, R.R. 1, Box 400, US 7, South Wallingford, VT 05773 (802–446–2611).

> Once a stagecoach stop, this 1792 building offers comfortable, simple lodging in a relaxing environment. Breakfasts are included, and lunches are available too.

Camping

Emerald Lake State Park, North Dorset, VT 05251.

> Picnic tables and fireplaces, fishing, rental boats and canoes, hiking, nature trails, tent and trailer sites, and hot showers.

Lake St. Catherine State Park, Poultney, VT 05764.

> Picnic tables and fireplaces, fishing, rental boats, hiking, nature trail, nature museum, playground, tent and trailer sites, lean-tos, and hot showers.

Bicycle Service

Battenkill, Inc., Intersection of US 7 and VT 11–30, Manchester, VT (802–362–2734).

First Stop Ski & Bike Shop, HCR34, Routes 4 & 100 South, Killington, VT (802–422–9050).

Great Outdoors Trading, 41 Center Street, Rutland, VT (802–775–6531).

Green Mountain Schwinn Cyclery, 133 Strongs Avenue, Rutland, VT (802–775–0869). Sales, service, rentals.

Mountain Cycology, Lamere Square, P.O. Box 527, Ludlow VT (802–228–2722).

Sports Peddlar, 158 North Main Street, Rutland, VT (802–775–0102). Sales, service.

Central Vermont

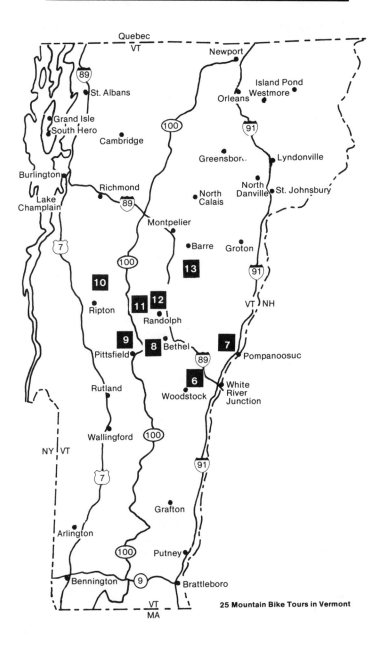

Quebec
VT

Newport

89

St. Albans

Island Pond
Westmore
Orleans

Grand Isle
South Hero

100

Cambridge

Greensboro
Lyndonville

91

Burlington

Richmond

89

Lake
Champlain

North
Calais

North
Danville
St. Johnsbury

Montpelier

7

Barre
Groton

13

100

91

10

Ripton

11 **12**

Randolph

VT NH

9 **8** Bethel

7

Pittsfield

89

Pompanoosuc

6

Woodstock

White
River
Junction

Rutland

NY VT

100

Wallingford

91

7

Grafton

Arlington

100

Putney

Bennington

9

Brattleboro

VT
MA

25 Mountain Bike Tours in Vermont

Woodstock

Distance: 8.9 miles
Difficulty: Easy
Riding surface: About 2/3 gravel, 1/3 pavement
Towns included: Woodstock, Hartford, Pomfret
Maps: USGS 7.5' Woodstock North, Quechee

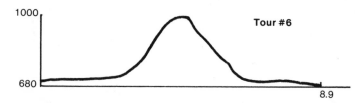

Woodstock is one of Vermont's best preserved and most elegant towns. Settled in 1765, the town became the county seat or Shire Town twenty years later, and it enjoyed vigorous early growth and commercial success. Today, the well-kept village houses and those in the surrounding hills are fine examples of the gracious architecture of the past.

Three former residents are often credited with making the greatest contributions to the environmental and historic preservation of Woodstock. George Perkins Marsh was a native son who became a congressman, a principle founder of the Smithsonian Museum, and the first internationally recognized conservationist after the publication of his book, *Man and Nature.* The environmental ethic upon which the book was based had its roots in the hills around Woodstock, where Marsh first studied nature and noted with dismay that large-scale land clearing resulted in more water run-off. The extra run-off was creating soil erosion and damaging stream ecosystems.

Frederick Billings, the builder of the Northern Pacific Railroad, later purchased the Marsh homestead and inspired the reforestation of the surrounding hills. The Marsh-Billings estate was subsequently occupied by Billings' granddaughter Mary Rockefeller and her husband. They have carried on the tradition of environmentalism and have helped the town retain its charm and beauty by encouraging the concept of appropriate commercial scale.

There are a variety of things to see and do in Woodstock in conjunction with this tour, and your mountain bike is a good way to get around. The Billings Farm and Museum at which this trip begins and ends is a

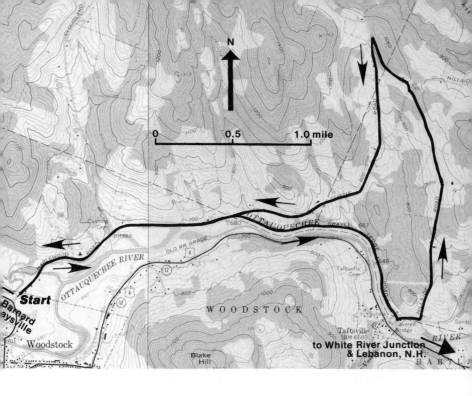

working dairy farm, as well as an excellent museum of early New England agricultural life, and is a fitting counterpoint to your excursion by bicycle into the surrounding hills. Mr. Billings established the bloodline of the registered Jersey herd in 1872, and milking is done twice a day in the modern, spotless milking parlor that is open to the public. Sheep, work horses, and oxen are also on the premises.

The museum features many exhibits of tools, utensils, machines, sleighs, and household goods from the past. Many displays employ large photographs or illustrations as backdrops to show how items were actually used. Special demonstrations are held during the year as well, when you can try your hand at making butter or cider, or watch a skilled artisan carve duck decoys out of butternut. The League of New Hampshire Wheelmen frequently includes the museum on its summer itinerary of places where their members show and demonstrate their wonderful collection of antique bicycles.

Also worth a side trip is the Vermont Institute of Natural Science (VINS), a research and education center that operates programs statewide. Located on a seventy-seven-acre nature preserve, VINS offers self-guided nature tours, bird banding demonstrations, lectures, and trips. The Vermont Raptor Center is also on the premises, a living museum and rehabilitation facility for over forty birds of prey that specializes in the needs and habitat of owls and hawks.

0.0 Begin at the entrance to the parking lot of the Billings Farm Museum, with the museum on your right, and proceed straight ahead on the River Road (called Maplewood Road on the USGS maps).

You are likely to encounter other bicyclists on this road. Because it by-passes busy US 4 on the opposite side of the river, and because its hard gravel surface is suitable for standard ten-speed road bikes, it is a popular bicycle conduit to the neighboring town of Quechee.

0.8 Pass a cemetery on the left; here the paved surface gives way to gravel.

Although the country cemeteries such as this one that dot Vermont's landscape seem to exude the peace and tranquility you would expect of "a final resting place," they were in the past regularly the scene of ghoulish nocturnal activity. During the first half of the nineteenth century, professional grave robbers regularly absconded with newly buried corpses and sold them as specimens for dissection to local medical schools — one of them located here in Woodstock. Being outside the village, cemeteries such as this one could be visited with less chance of detection.

An offense punishable by fine, imprisonment, or whipping, grave robbing was its own industry replete with tradesmen skilled in the clandestine disinterment of bodies. Using a system developed through years of practice, grave robbers are thought to have been able to complete a job in little more than an hour and leave little trace for eventual detection. In fact, apprehensions for the crime were virtually unheard of, even though it is estimated that several hundred corpses were dug up and sold.

1.5 Pass the Rivendell Farm.

1.7 Bear RIGHT.

The Ottauquechee River parallels the road on your right and is a popular recreational resource during the summer. Canoes float by in the spring and early summer, and when hot summer days arrive, a lazy float in an inner tube is a sure way to keep cool. Fly fishermen enjoy persuading the river's wary brook, brown, and rainbow trout to sample their feathered inventions.

2.5 Continue STRAIGHT past a road to the left.

2.9 Keep to the RIGHT.

3.2 Turn LEFT at Taftsville Covered Bridge, pass the Taftsville Tea House on the right, and climb the steep but brief incline.

The Taftsville Covered Bridge on your right was built in 1836 and, along with the hydro dam waterfall it overlooks, is a popular backdrop for tourist photographers. Across the bridge on heavily traveled US 4 is the Taftsville Country Store, a community grocery in business for fifty years. They have an extensive selection of Vermont food products on the premises and have offered mail order catalog shopping for thirty years.

3.3 Turn LEFT onto Hillside Road and begin a considerable climb.

3.6 Good views to the south behind you.

4.0 Good views to the west on your left.

4.9 Keep to the LEFT at this intersection.

5.3 Take a sharp LEFT.

6.0 Keep to the RIGHT past Phoenix Road on the left.

6.4 Continue STRAIGHT past another road on the left and begin a steep but brief climb.

7.2 Bear RIGHT onto the same road (River Road) on which you began the trip and continue STRAIGHT ahead back to the Farm Museum parking lot.

8.9 You are back at the Billings Farm Museum parking lot.

Woodstock cyclists at the turn of the century are proof that cycling has long been a popular pastime.

Accommodations

The Kedron Valley Inn, VT 106, South Woodstock, VT 05071 (802–457–1473).
Canopy beds, Franklin fireplaces, and antique quilts give this inn an authentic nineteenth-century flavor. The food is great, there's a big pond for swimming, and it's adjacent to Kedron Valley Stables if you'd like to ride something with legs instead of wheels.

Three Church Street, 3 Church Street, Woodstock, VT 05091 (802–457–1925).
A bed and breakfast establishment in a fine old Federal house near the green that includes a swimming pool and tennis court. Dinner as well by arrangement.

Camping

Silver Lake State Park, Barnard, VT 05031.
Picnic tables and fireplaces, swimming, fishing, tent sites, lean-tos, trailer sites, and hot showers.

White River Valley Camping, Gaysville, VT 05746.
Riverside campsites, log cabin lodge, congenial atmosphere, full services. Whirlpool spa, weight room, rec hall, store, laundry. Open all year.

Bicycle Service

The Cyclery Plus, US 4, West Woodstock, VT (802–457–3377). Sales, service.

Woodstock Sports, 30 Central Street, Woodstock, VT (802–457–1568). Sales, service, rentals.

7

Norwich

Distance: 21 miles
Difficulty: Moderate/Strenuous
Riding surface: Mostly gravel, with small amount of pavement
Towns included: Norwich, Thetford
Maps: USGS 7.5' South Strafford, Lyme (NH)

0.0   Begin at the junction of VT 132 and US 5. Proceed WEST on VT 132 under the I-89 overpass. On the left is the mouth of the Ompompanoosuc River, where this picturesque stream enters the larger Connecticut River.

0.7   Turn RIGHT at the fork onto the gravel road.

0.9   Turn LEFT at the intersection, onto the road marked by a sign as "Campbell Flats." The fields on the left on this stretch are planted with asparagus and raspberries.

2.3   Turn LEFT at the intersection. Looking straight ahead at the horizon, you can see the top of the Union Village Dam in the distance.
   Just beyond this intersection on a sunny afternoon in June, I came across a small, spotted fawn in the middle of the road. Not knowing what to make of my silent, wheeled intrusion, the fawn hesitated uncertainly, performing a nervous dance in the road. Suddenly, as if on cue, the fawn dove into the brush with a tremendous leap. After passing the spot, I glanced over my shoulder at another sound of crashing brush and saw the large doe bound across the road after her young one.

2.8   On your left, you'll pass the Thetford town boundary marker.

3.0   Turn LEFT, cross the covered bridge, and then turn RIGHT.
   The Union Village covered bridge you have just crossed was built in 1867 and is about one hundred feet in length. It is built with a

"multiple kingpost" structural design. The kingpost truss is one of the most basic in covered bridge design and can be identified by the beams along the walls that look like large inverted "V's" (the compression pieces), with an upright beam in the middle (the kingpost). This same truss concept was employed to give added structural strength in nineteenth-century barns as well.

Proceed straight ahead toward the Union Village Dam. Climb the paved access road and cross the top of the dam.

When you first contrast the magnitude of the Union Village Dam to the gentle Ompompanoosuc that flows through the dam's gates, it seems like a case of overkill by the U.S. Army Corps of Engineers. A fifth of a mile long and 170-feet high, the dam seems more appropriate for a river much larger than this. However, this dam is really part of a flood control strategy to minimize flood damage in the Connecticut River Basin many miles downstream. According to the engineers, this dam cost just over four million dollars at the time it was built between 1947 and 1950. If a major flood equal to that of 1936 were to occur, the dam would prevent nearly seven million dollars in damages. I can't explain how they calculated that though.

In any event, this is a big dam. Nearly two million cubic yards of fill and seventeen thousand cubic yards of concrete went into its construction. Its drainage area is 126 square miles, and the reservoir capacity covers 720 acres. When full, it can hold more than twelve billion gallons of water. It is currently managed as a recreational facility for picnicking, bathing, fishing, and hiking.

3.9 Turn LEFT on the far side of the gatehouse and continue for about 3 miles until you reach VT 113 in Thetford Center. Note the "high water mark" signs just downhill from the gatehouse.

4.6 On your right pass Union Village Dam nature trails of 2.5 and 1.3 miles. The trails are restricted to hikers.

If you wish to hike one of the trails as a diversion, be sure to lock your bicycle.

5.8 On your left is a pleasant picnic area next to the river, where a wooden footbridge crosses to another nature trail, The Mystery Trail. Again, the trail is open to hikers only.

6.3 Pass another picnic area on your left.

6.8 Turn LEFT onto VT 113 and pass through the village of Thetford Center. The village store is on the right next to the Methodist Church.

8.1 Turn RIGHT onto "Five Corners Road" and prepare to climb. Continue on this road for 2.5 miles.

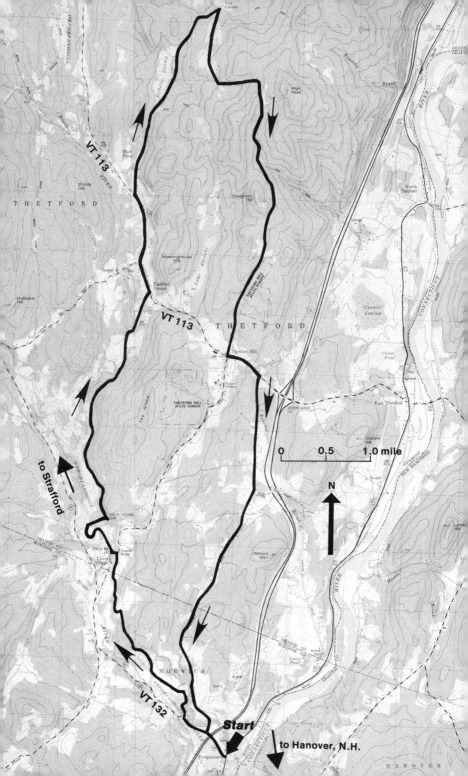

to Strafford

VT 113

VT 113

THETFORD

VT 132

to Hanover, N.H.

Start

N

0   0.5   1.0 mile

Local opinion joins distance and direction to make this a unique impromptu sign.

10.6 Turn RIGHT at the intersection. Continue on this road for nearly 5 miles until you once again meet VT 113.

15.4 Turn LEFT onto VT 113, travel a short distance, and take the first paved road on the right. This road turns to gravel before too long and returns you to the starting point in about 4.5 miles. You'll be able to see I-89 off in the distance to the left for the first mile or so on this road.

19.1 Pass the Thetford-Norwich town line.
There are several private ponds near the residences along this road that represent a different approach to water containment than that used in the Union Village Dam. Actually, there are many small man-made ponds through much of the state, usually under an acre in size. Most people stock them with a few trout, swim in them, skate on them, and use them for watering livestock. Fortunately for Vermont pond builders, the state has an excellent subsoil for building ponds. It compacts well and is not too porous. There is also an abundance of springs throughout the state to supply the water. The process for building such ponds is relatively simple. A bulldozer first clears the area of topsoil, which may vary from a few inches deep to a foot or two. The pond basin is then carved out to a depth of eight or ten feet, and the material removed is piled along the edge to become the dam. Finally, the bulldozer shapes and compacts the new dam and finishes by spreading the previously removed topsoil along the outside of the dam so that grass will grow. If all goes well, the new pond will fill with water in a few weeks.

20.0 Bear LEFT.

20.7 This is the intersection with VT 132. Turn LEFT.

21.0 This is the intersection with US 5 where the trip began.

Accommodations
The Stone House Inn, Box 47, US 5, Thetford, VT 05054 (802–333–9124).
Located on the banks of the Connecticut River, this 1835 stone farmhouse offers six comfortable rooms and is open year-round. In the summer, this inn is part of an inn-to-inn canoeing package.

Camping
None nearby

Bicycle Service
The Brick Store Bicycles, On The Green, Strafford, VT (802–765–4441). Sales, service.
Omer and Bob's, 7 Allen Street, Hanover, NH (603–643–3525). Sales, service.

8

Bethel

Distance: 18.4 miles
Difficulty: Moderate
Riding surface: Primarily maintained gravel roads, some forest trail, a small stretch of pavement
Towns included: Bethel, Gaysville, Stockbridge
Map: USGS 7.5' Bethel

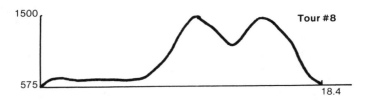

Much of the first third of this trip meanders close by the west bank of the beautiful White River; then, a climb into the rolling "hill country" offers an interesting contrast. The final four miles is a demanding forest trail; however, there is an easier alternative route that is a relatively flat retracing of the trip's beginning. The first portion of the trip can be done as an out-and-back excursion that is well suited for children and beginners.

Bethel claims the distinction of being the first town chartered by the independent Republic of Vermont, the matter being finalized two days before Christmas in 1779. This area was still a frontier at the time. The settling of the town was delayed for a couple of years by apprehension brought on by an Indian raid that wiped out the neighboring town of Royalton. At least one of the early Bethel settlers was taken prisoner by Indians while clearing land.

With good land and ample water power, the community was prospering by the 1830s. The original town saw and grist mill is still operating today under the name of Bethel Mills after nearly two hundred years. It is the longest continuously operated business in the state and still supplies area residents with animal feed and building supplies.

Bethel also has a tradition of granite quarrying. Around the turn of the century, quarrying the rare "Bethel White" granite was begun on the northern end of town at a location still visible from the southbound lane of Vermont I-89, just before Exit 3. Nearly three hundred workers were employed in Bethel's granite industry at its peak, including many skilled and well-paid Italian immigrant craftsmen. Bethel granite has been used in the construction of public buildings throughout the United States, and quarrying on a small scale continues.

Also around the turn of the century, the state's largest tannery with 150 employees was located in Bethel, but two disastrous fires and increased competition from tanneries using newly discovered chemical processes spelled the end of this business.

The first passenger train to penetrate the interior of Vermont made its maiden voyage from White River Junction to Bethel in June of 1848. Today, Bethel has a stable population of around eighteen hundred and is home to a variety of manufacturing enterprises, including a plastics factory, a small furniture plant, a national wire broker, and the Vermont Castings' wood stove assembly plant.

0.0 Park your vehicle in the lot at the north end of Bethel's Main Street, the original location of the Bethel Inn. Begin the trip in front of Richardson's Store, with the store on your left.

> On your right note the old railroad depot building and, just up the street, the Bethel library where an interesting etching on the wall inside graphically portrays the suffering endured at Andersonville Prison during the Civil War.

Proceed, passing Dean's Mobil on your right, and bear RIGHT at the intersection of VT 12 and VT 107. Pass under the overpass and make an immediate sharp RIGHT. Remain on this road for the next 6 miles or so until you reach the Gaysville Bridge.

1.3 With the Long Meadow Farm on your right, continue STRAIGHT ahead.

2.1 Pass the Washburn house, built in 1794 and believed to be Bethel's oldest standing building still in use, on your left.

> This section of Bethel was the part of town originally settled. Situated along the White River that flows to your left, this area had rich soil for growing crops and a ready source of water from the adjacent river. The river was probably also used as a transportation route by Indians, which may explain why early settler David Stone was captured by Indians while clearing land along its banks.

2.5 The modern facility across the river is the White River National Fish Hatchery. Although it is not possible "to get there from here," the hatchery has a visitor center with displays explaining the salmon restoration project. The entrance to the facility is located a couple of miles south of Bethel on VT 107.

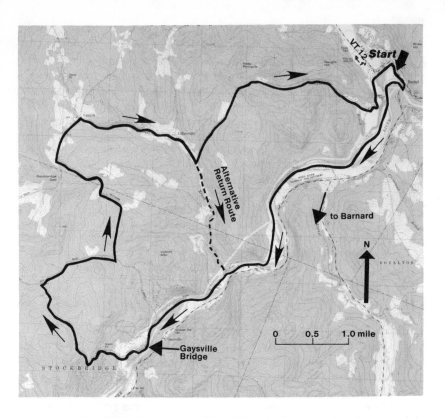

The White River is considered an ideal salmon river because it is clear, clean, and has no dams. The river was once, as were many of the tributaries of the Connecticut River, a recipient of large runs of Atlantic salmon, many of which weighed more than forty pounds. With the building of a dam in South Hadley, Massachusetts, in 1797, the salmon were cut off from their spawning grounds, and the runs ended.

Today, great strides have been made in restoring the salmon runs of the past. Pollution control facilities and fish ladders have been constructed in crucial areas downstream, and the White River National Fish Hatchery was designed to raise millions of salmon annually for release.

In the summer of 1986, a sea run Atlantic salmon was found in the White River just upstream from here. It was the first salmon to have returned to this section of the river in nearly two hundred years and is hopefully a sign that the salmon restoration program will be successful.

The river also offers excellent fly-fishing for rainbow and brown trout, with many several pounders being landed by skilled fishermen each year.

4.5 Continue straight past the Lilliesville Road on the right, and shortly after, a cemetery and another road, also on the right.

6.1 Here the road turns briefly to pavement, and the Gaysville Bridge appears on the left. Although the tour continues past the bridge without crossing it, you will find this a worthwhile spot to linger. The White River Camping Area is located just on the other side of the bridge, and the deep pool below the bridge is a popular summer swimming hole.

Few Vermont towns were ravaged as viciously by the flood of 1927 as was Gaysville. This thriving little community was virtually swept away on November 5 of that flood year, a victim of the same river that had played such an important role in the town's commercial success. Such was the power of that mighty flood that the river actually changed course, carving an ugly swath for its new bed a few hundred feet to the west. The original channel is overgrown with brush but is still visible on the VT 107 side of the post office and on the opposite side of the road.

6.3 Continuing past the bridge, pass the Cobblehouse Inn on your left and bear LEFT at the fork.

6.5 Bear RIGHT at this fork, and prepare for the trip's first major ascent, a precipitously steep and rough challenge. Most cyclists will walk up at least part of the hill. Pass the Laolke Lodge on your right, and a short distance later, a gravel pit, also on your right.

7.4 Pass the White River Works, on the right.

This small business is a highly sophisticated manufacturing shop that produces custom wood products for architects and the general building trade. If you need a reproduction of antique wooden moldings no longer made, kitchen cabinets, or nearly any other finely finished wood product, the White River Works can make it to your specifications.

7.5 At this intersection with a private road to the left, bear RIGHT. At this point and for the next mile, the road becomes a trail through woods.

8.6 Turn RIGHT at this intersection onto Lyon Hill Road and begin a gradual climb.

9.7 Turn LEFT onto the gravel Whitcomb Hill Road.

11.0 Bear LEFT at the intersection.

11.2 Continue STRAIGHT.

11.7 Turn RIGHT onto Gay Hill Road, with a cemetery appearing on your right. If you are planning to stop for lunch, this peaceful spot is a good place, for the next 3 miles are an exhilarating downhill run.

12.4   Having just passed the Bethel Lympus Church, circa 1830, turn RIGHT onto the Lilliesville Road.

13.8   Pass a road on your left, as well as an attractive house built around 1830.

14.3   Turn LEFT onto this road, which will take you back to the starting point. Watch carefully for this turn, for the entrance can be easy to miss. The rusted remains of two antique vehicles can be seen in the weeds off to the side, and the road rises sharply into the forest. The road may not be in the best repair, and since it consists of a very steep climb and then an equally steep descent, some portions may require walking.

> **Alternate route:** For a less demanding but less interesting return trip, pass by this turnoff and continue straight to the River Road intersection that you passed on the first portion of the trip. Turn LEFT and continue straight to retrace the first 4.5 miles of the trip, back to your starting point.

14.7   Keep to the LEFT.

15.0   Here you'll pass a camp on the right and the remains of a barn on the left. Continue STRAIGHT on the trail as it becomes less visible.

15.4   Continue STRAIGHT.

17.2   Continue STRAIGHT.

17.5   Bear LEFT at this intersection.

17.6   Here pavement begins, and you pass the town garage on your right.

18.0   Keep to the RIGHT at this intersection with VT 12.

18.3   Bear RIGHT after crossing the bridge.

18.4   Arrive back at your vehicle parking area.

Beginner's Trip

The first portion of this trip is an excellent ride of just over 12 miles for those with children or for those desiring a less strenuous trip. Follow the directions to the 6.1-mile mark at the Gaysville Bridge, enjoy a picnic there if you wish, and retrace the route back to Bethel.

Accommodations
Greenhurst Inn, RD 2, Box 60, Bethel, VT (802–234–9474).
> Elegant Victorian decor with tennis court, gazebo, croquet on premises.

Camping
Silver Lake State Park, Barnard, VT 05031.
> Picnic tables and fireplaces, swimming, fishing, tent sites, lean-tos, trailer sites, and hot showers.

The stately maples of this unoccupied Bethel farm continue to supply sap via plastic tubing to a neighboring sugar maker.

White River Valley Camping, Gaysville, VT 05746.
  Riverside campsites, log cabin lodge, congenial atmosphere, full services.
  Whirlpool spa, weight room, rec hall, store, laundry. Open all year.

Bicycle Service

The Cyclery Plus, US 4, West Woodstock, VT (fifteen miles from starting point)
  (802–457–3377). Sales, service.
Green Mountain Bicycle Service, P.O. Box 253, Rte. 100, Rochester, VT (ten
  miles from starting point) (802–767–4464). Sales, service, rentals, tours.
New England Bicycle Tours, 41 S. Main Street, Randolph, VT (ten miles from
  starting point) (802–728–3261). Rentals, tours.
Woodstock Sports, 30 Central Street, Woodstock, VT (fifteen miles from starting
  point) (802–457–1568). Sales, service, rentals.

Pittsfield

Distance: 15 miles
Difficulty: Moderate
Riding surface: A good mix of forest trail and gravel, with a small amount of pavement
Towns included: Pittsfield, Rochester
Map: USGS 7.5' Rochester

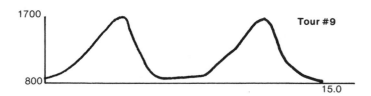

With its central green complete with gazebo, Pittsfield is a living reminder of Vermont villages of the past. Settlement began in the early 1790s with the establishment of the essential industries of frontier life: a sawmill for producing lumber for houses and barns, and a gristmill for converting corn and field grains to flour. The town itself was named after Pittsfield, Massachusetts.

Late in the last century, Pittsfield had a bicycle rim factory engaged in making wooden rims. One hundred years ago when wood was plentiful, inexpensive, and the technology for working with it had reached its peak, wood was the common material for rims. A Pittsfield man even invented a special bicycle he called a "snow cycle" for winter riding. This interesting contraption featured a single-runner blade in place of the front wheel. Instead of the standard rear wheel there was a tubeless rim with pairs of double metal spikes mounted at five-inch intervals. The rider pedaled, the rear rim turned, the spikes dug in, and away you went. If the village library is open when you are there, stop by and take a look at the local history book. Page 134 pictures this snow cycle.

Today, the tradition of cycling in Pittsfield is alive and well in the form of Vermont Mountain Bike Tours, headquartered at The Pittsfield Inn. Here you can join one of Tom Yennerell's guided tours of the surrounding area. The tours are geared as much as possible to rider ability and include the rental of a high-quality bike, a helmet, a water bottle (that you get to keep), and instruction as required. For guests of the inn, self-

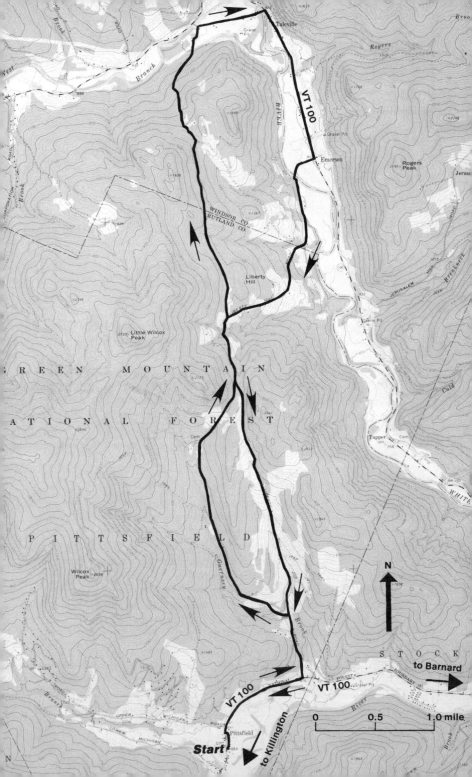

guided tours are available that include breakfast, dinner, and a guide map in addition to equipment and lodging. For more information, including prices, contact Tom Yennerell at Vermont Mountain Bike Tours, P.O. Box 541–B, Pittsfield, Vermont 05762, or call 802–746–8580.

0.0 The journey begins at the gazebo on the village green. With the gazebo on your left, follow the road around the green and turn right onto VT 100, heading east. Continue on VT 100 for nearly a mile, passing on your left first the "100's Rainbow" gift and craft shop, then the Swiss Farm Lodge.

0.9 Just past the Colton Farm (labeled with a sign in front), turn LEFT onto the Liberty Hill Road and prepare for a brief initial climb.
    The Liberty Hill Road was an important early route for settlers in the area, linking Pittsfield with the town of Rochester. It is believed to have been laid out before 1800.

1.4 Turn LEFT at the fork in the road, and prepare for a good climb of a half mile or so.
    As you make the climb, you'll hear Guernsey Brook gurgling pleasantly in the woods to the left. This lively little stream was named not as you might imagine for the handsome cows of that bovine breed but for a local nineteenth-century entrepreneur. A. P. Guernsey owned and operated a sawmill and a gristmill powered by the brook until the 1880s when a flood washed out the dam. Horses are now kept in the field to the left. Also note the large number of wild apple trees along either side of the road, a feature that graces much of the first half of the trip. When the apples ripen in the early fall, keep an eye out for deer and ruffed grouse.

3.2 Bear RIGHT at this fork and climb once again.
    If you are making this trip near the middle of August, you might want to take a quarter-mile side trip down the road to the left to sample the blackberries that can be found there. Don't forget to take into account any side trips in your odometer reading.

3.9 Keep to the LEFT at this intersection.

4.5 Bear LEFT at this intersection and begin a slight climb. The road to the right plunges downhill, and a camp proclaimed by its sign to be "Spike Horn Lodge" lies between the two roads.
    "Going to camp" is a valued tradition for the Vermont deer hunters fortunate enough to own one. Most camps are sparsely furnished like this one and are typically used only during the two or three weeks of deer hunting season in November. Evenings around a wood stove with the comradery of good friends, exaggerated recollections of past hunting accomplishments, and perhaps some fresh venison have provided cherished memories for generations of Vermont hunters.

Given that a "spike horn" is a young male deer and that the hunter's usual quest is the massive old trophy buck, the name of this lodge may be a humorous reference to its hunters' success rate.

5.0 Continue past this sturdy forest service barricade telling you that the road ahead is closed to motor vehicles because of a "soft road bed." The road poses no problems for a mountain bike.

5.8 Here the road ends abruptly. Continue straight ahead, onto the barely visible trail entering the woods. Blowdowns immediately block the trail, but a short detour on the left will lead you around the problem. Be careful as you gradually descend this trail, for it is deeply rutted and quite overgrown with grass.

6.1 Continue STRAIGHT ahead past another forest trail leading off to the right.

6.2 Bear LEFT as the trail again joins a gravel road, and prepare for a steep and somewhat rough descent.

6.9 Go around this second barricade prohibiting motor vehicles.

7.0 Continue straight past a cluster of houses on both sides as the road emerges from the forest, glide down the slight grade, passing the District #4 State Highway garage on your right, and cross the steel bridge over the White River to reach VT 100 south of Rochester Village.

This section of Rochester carries the name "Talcville" from the past century when talc was mined in the surrounding area and processed in a facility near this spot. Talc in a compact form is better known as soapstone, famous for its heat-retention powers and its ability to be shaped. The more powdery talc had a variety of applications in the olden days and was an ingredient in paper, tires, and cosmetics.

7.7 Turn RIGHT onto VT 100.

9.1 Turn RIGHT onto the Liberty Hill Road (the opposite end of the road that you entered near the beginning of the trip), cross the river once again, pass the Liberty Hill Farm, and prepare for a final major climb.

The Liberty Hill Farm is a large working dairy farm, but it offers five guest rooms as well. The owners welcome families, and meals are served family style with everything made from scratch.

There are extremely good views to the south as you make this ascent, and part way up you'll pass a gorgeous and distinctive residence recognized by the matching red roofs of house, barn, and gazebo. Still farther, you'll pass several camps on the left.

10.9 Turn LEFT, with the Spike Horn Lodge encountered earlier on the right.

An abandoned, horse-drawn hay rake commands an impressive view in Pittsfield.

For about the next 1.5 miles you will be retracing the path you traveled previously.

11.5 Turn LEFT at this intersection, leaving the road you arrived on as it goes to the right. After a brief climb, you'll enjoy a pleasant descent of nearly 2 miles, with a spectacular view to the right. Along the roadside near the top is a good place to picnic.

12.5 Continue STRAIGHT, past a road on the left and an adjacent camp with a moose motif, also on the left.

13.4 Keep to the RIGHT at the intersection.

13.6 Bear LEFT at the intersection and rejoin the road you traveled on at the beginning of the trip.

14.1 Turn RIGHT onto VT 100, heading back toward the village of Pittsfield.

15.0 Arrive back at your departure point, the gazebo.

Accommodations
The Pittsfield Inn, Box 526, Pittsfield, VT 05762 (802–746–8943).
> Ten recently restored guest rooms that are individually decorated with antiques, quilts, and period wallpapers are featured by this classic country inn. A large expanse of lawn for evening strolls or games, a renowned kitchen, and an inviting dining room combine for an elegant and relaxing ambiance.

Swiss Farm Lodge, VT 100 North, Pittsfield, VT 05762 (802–746–8341).
> This bed & breakfast is a working beef farm that features a friendly home atmosphere, private baths, a lounge with fireplace, and home cooking served family style. They make their own maple syrup, honey, and jams.

Camping
Silver Lake State Park, Barnard, VT 05031.
> Picnic tables and fireplaces, swimming, fishing, tent sites, trailer sites, and hot showers.

Gifford Woods State Park, Killington, VT 05751.
> Picnicking, tent sites, trailer sites, hot showers, foot trails.

White River Valley Camping, Gaysville, VT 05746.
> Riverside campsites, log cabin lodge, congenial atmosphere, full services. Whirlpool spa, weight room, rec hall, store, laundry. Open all year.

Bicycle Service
The Cyclery Plus, US 4, West Woodstock, VT (ten miles from starting point) (802–457–3377). Sales, service.

Green Mountain Bicycle Service, P.O. Box 253, Route 100, Rochester, VT (fifteen miles from starting point) (802–767–4464). Sales, service, rentals, tours.

Green Mountain Schwinn Cyclery, 133 Strongs Avenue, Rutland, VT (fifteen miles from starting point) (802–775–0869). Sales, service, rentals.

Woodstock Sports, 30 Central Street, Woodstock, VT (ten miles from starting point) (802–457–1568). Sales, service, rentals.

10

Ripton

Distance: 14.9 miles, 29.8 miles round trip
Difficulty: Moderate/Strenuous
Riding surface: Primarily gravel, with some pavement
Towns included: Ripton, Lincoln
Maps: USGS 7.5' Bread Loaf, Lincoln

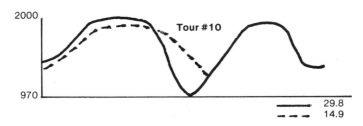

Poet Robert Frost spent many summers in Ripton enjoying the solitude of the forest and the beauty of the mountains, along with teaching at the Bread Loaf School of English. The starting point for this trip is the Robert Frost Wayside, a highway rest and picnic area on VT 125. A half-mile road next to the wayside leads up to the farmhouse in which Frost stayed for many summers. A half mile in the opposite direction leads to the Robert Frost Interpretive Nature Trail, worth visiting. Designed for walking and not for bikes, the interpretive trail identifies a variety of local flora and features stations displaying appropriate Frost poems for each particular view.

Although born in California and having lived in Massachusetts, New Hampshire, and Bennington, Vermont, Frost developed an affection for the Ripton area that area residents reciprocated.

0.0 Start from the Robert Frost Wayside area on VT 125. With the picnic tables and privies on your left, proceed on VT 125. Pass a road on the left almost as soon as you leave the wayside.

This road on the left climbs a slight grade for a half mile to the farmhouse in which poet Robert Frost spent his summers, and makes a good side trip upon your return. You can make the side trip first, but note that the mileage directions here do not include this extra mile.

0.5 Turn LEFT onto the National Forest Service road, marked by brown signs with white lettering.

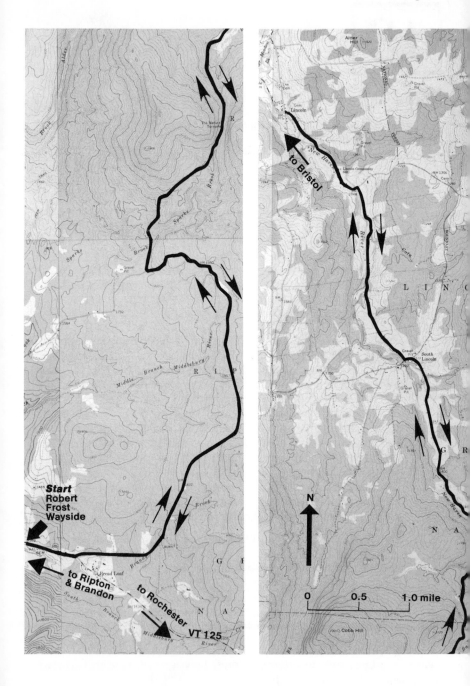

Start
Robert
Frost
Wayside

to Ripton
& Brandon

to Rochester
VT 125

to Bristol

N

0   0.5   1.0 mile

0.7 Pass on the right the back side of Middlebury College's Bread Loaf Campus.

This attractive facility is worth viewing from the front at the conclusion of this trip. Originally a vacation resort called the Bread Loaf Inn, the complex was willed to Middlebury College in 1915 upon innkeeper Joseph Battell's death. Today, Middlebury College's Bread Loaf School of English attracts distinguished writers and teachers for the summer sessions.

Joseph Battell was as magnanimous during his life as after his death. Not a native of Ripton, Battell first came to the area on his doctor's orders for a recuperative vacation of clean mountain air to strengthen his weak lungs. A weekend of mountain serenity was enough to convince Battell that this was a place worth permanent residency.

He established the Bread Loaf Inn in 1866, a freewheeling vacation spot that featured a huge dining hall, a hothouse for forcing vegetables, a bowling alley, a dance hall, and a target range, along with more typical recreational pastimes such as hiking, fishing, and porch-sitting. The inn was the first in Vermont to offer winter as well as summer vacations, and innkeeper Battell would frequently drive a sleigh over the snow-packed road twelve miles to Middlebury to pick up guests. Because he was independently wealthy thanks to an inheritance and a profitable publishing venture, Joseph Battell was able to concentrate on pleasing his guests rather than on making a profit.

He eventually became convinced that the surrounding forests would be ruined by logging and set out to buy land in huge tracts as a way of protecting it. At the time of his death he owned more than forty thousand acres, purchased for between 10¢ and $1.25 an acre, which he donated as well. Today much of that land is part of the Green Mountain National Forest.

In addition to being a writer, publisher, and innkeeper without comparison, Joseph Battell was a breeder of fine Morgan horses. The nearby Weybridge Horse Farm continues his work with many fine registered Morgans. He was an avid horticulturist, with a fine flower garden as well as an extensive vegetable enterprise. The Battell Biological Preserve in nearby Middlebury is a four hundred-acre monument to his interest in conservation. He was against the sale of liquor, favoring lemonade as a stimulating drink.

His love of horses and mountain serenity made Battell the state's staunchest opponent to the automobile. In his effort to dampen the interest of local residents in automobiles, for several years before his death he devoted a page of his Middlebury newspaper to grisly reports of automobile accidents all over the country.

0.9   Continue STRAIGHT past a road on the left.

1.2   Pass on your left a Bread Loaf Campus building named Gilmore.

1.5   Pass on the right a private road.

1.6   Pass on the right a sign for the "Burnt Hill Norske Trail."

1.9   Pass on the right a sign saying "Green Mountain National Forest."

2.3   Pass on the left a trail prohibiting motor vehicles but inviting hikers and cross-country skiers.

3.2   Pass on the left two trails in quick succession.

4.2   Pass on the right a directional sign for the Skylight Pond Trail and Skylight Lodge.

> Just after the sign, you'll come to a meadow that is maintained by the forest service as a wildlife feeding area. According to the information provided by a sign on the site, this was at one time the location of a sawmill. In 1969 the land was disked, fertilized, and seeded to provide food for wildlife. Apparently it is one of many areas in the National Forest that is maintained as a designated feeding area.

5.3   Turn RIGHT at this three-way intersection that has a large island in the center and several National Forest directional signs.

5.6   Cross Sparks Brook.

5.8   Bear RIGHT and remain on Forest Highway 54.

6.4   The Vermont Presidential Range of mountains comes into view on your right.

7.4   Arrive at a large, attractive beaver pond on your right. This is the turn-around point for the shorter version of this trip and is a nice spot for a picnic or rest before turning back. If you're planning the longer version, the next 7 miles or so to the village of Lincoln results in a net drop in elevation, so the return is mostly a gradual climb, with a couple of steeper climbs.

> This beaver pond offers a good view of typical beaver habitat.
> Beavers played a significant role in the settling of North America. Valued in the 1700s and 1800s for their skins, millions of beavers were trapped to supply the haberdasheries of England and France. Trappers could earn between ten and twenty dollars a day at a time when a farmer might earn only fifty cents in a day. Beavers were also prized as a source of castoreum, an ingredient for cure-alls and a base for cosmetic perfumes. Beavers produce castoreum in their glands to waterproof their fur and to mark their territories.

Beavers in Vermont ponds such as this one will weigh around fifty pounds and be about four-feet long. One of the largest beavers ever caught weighed 110 pounds.

A beaver colony usually consists of the mother and father, the young born the previous year, and the offspring of two years ago. When a new litter is ready to be born in the early spring, the two-year olds will be driven away from the pond to establish their own colonies. This practice prevents overcrowding and thereby prolongs the food supply and minimizes the incidence of disease. The beavers leaving home generally head downstream to find mates and build new dams. Although they generally build nearby, beavers have been known to travel nearly 150 miles in seven months.

Working at night and using almost anything available, including wood, mud, grass, and rocks, a pair of beavers can build a sizable dam in less than a week. During dam construction, the crest of the dam is raised uniformly, and low spots are filled in as they develop. Dams as high as eighteen feet (in Wyoming) and as long as four thousand feet (New Hampshire) have been reported.

8.4   Pass on the right a road that leads to another beaver pond.

9.1   Pass on your left the Spruce Lodge camp as the road starts to drop. On your left is a deep ravine. At the bottom of the descent, the New Haven River meanders next to the road.

9.6   Pass on the right a National Forest sign for Forest Highway 201.

10.0   The land opens up on the right, and the route in the next couple of miles becomes flatter and more settled with houses as you get closer to the village. Lincoln Mountain looms prominently to the left.

11.6   Continue STRAIGHT past a road on the right.

11.8   Continue STRAIGHT past a road on the right.

11.9   Continue STRAIGHT past a road on the left.

12.7   The road becomes paved.

13.8   Turn LEFT at this intersection and cross the bridge over the New Haven River.

14.1   Pass on your right the Lincoln School.

14.7   Pass on your right the Long Run Inn.

14.9   You have arrived at the Lincoln General Store, and the turn-around for the longer version of this trip.

First settled in 1780, Lincoln is a beautiful town nearly enclosed by mountains and rugged hills. It lies on the west side of the Green

Mountain Range and is dominated by Mount Abraham at 4,052 feet. This eminent mountain is also known as Potatoe Hill. Lincoln Mountain, of which Mount Abraham is the southernmost peak, extends along the northeastern border of the town. The Presidential Range forms the southeastern border.

Many of the early settlers of this area were Quakers. By the mid 1800s, the population had reached fifteen hundred. Today there are about half that number living in Lincoln.

The New Haven River powered twelve mills in Lincoln alone during the 1800s. With an abundance of trees on the surrounding hills, Lincoln Lumber was for many years a large manufacturing concern in the village. The company made wooden butter tubs and wooden boxes, and records show an impressive production rate. In 1892 Lincoln Lumber produced nineteen thousand tubs; by 1899, the twenty-five men on the payroll turned out nearly a quarter million. For many years the company operated an acetyline carbide generator that produced enough extra gas to light the village store, the church, and several homes in the village.

Several agricultural commodities were exported from Lincoln in the early years. Potatoes were an important crop, and by 1824 the harvest exceeded twenty thousand bushels, a handsome supplement to the thirty thousand pounds of maple sugar boiled off and the nine thousand pounds of wool shorn that year. Almost one hundred years later, potatoes were still a valuable crop.

Not all of the work carried on in early Lincoln was hard and honest. An early entrepreneur of the town was Dr. J. S. Dodge who concocted and widely sold a variety of cure-all medicines. One of them was simply called "86" and was described as "The Best Genito-Urinary Tonic Known." Dr. Dodge claimed that "86" cured menstruation difficulties, chorea, prolapsed uterus, and sterility, that it prevented miscarriages, and that it was good for diseases of the bladder and kidneys.

Retrace the route exactly to return to the Robert Frost Wayside.

Accommodations

The Long Run Inn, R.D. 1, Box 560, Bristol, VT 05443 (802–453–3233).
    A country inn built in 1799 with a wrap-around porch overlooking the New Haven River, and Mount Abraham nearby. A variety of cuisines and an imaginative menu of meals home cooked by the innkeepers.
The Chipman Inn, VT 125, Ripton, VT 05766 (802–388–2390).
    A traditional Vermont inn in a beautiful village location with warm hospitality, fine food, wine and spirits for guests. Nine rooms, seven with private baths.

A Ripton beaver colony displays this fine example of their craft.

Camping
Branbury State Park, Brandon, VT 05733.
   Picnic tables and fireplaces, swimming, boating, fishing, hiking, tent sites, lean-tos, and hot showers.

Bicycle Service
Bike and Ski Touring Center, 74 Main Street, Middlebury, VT (ten miles from starting point) (802–388–6666). Sales, service.
Green Mountain Bicycle Service, P.O. Box 253, Route 100, Rochester, VT (fifteen miles from starting point) (802–767–4464). Sales, service, rentals, tours.
Mad River Bike Shop, Rt. 100, P.O. Box 871, Waitsfield, VT (802–496–9500).
Ski Haus, Merchants Row, Middlebury, VT (802–388–6762).

Braintree Gap

Distance: 26 miles
Difficulty: Strenuous
Riding surface: Extensive forest trail, some gravel, some pavement
Towns included: Braintree, Granville, Rochester
Maps: USGS 7.5' Hancock; USGS 15' Randolph

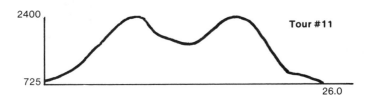

The departure point for this trip is the Seventh Day Adventist Church on VT 12A in Braintree. To reach it, take VT 12A north from Randolph Village for about 4 miles. On the side of the church is a picnic area sponsored by the Grange, with ample parking.

0.0 Leave the parking area and head north on VT 12A, passing the church on your left. Continue north on VT 12A, noting the inviting mountain range on your left that you will be crossing.

3.0 Turn LEFT onto a barely visible trail entering the woods, on the south side of a white house. At first glance it may appear that you will be riding across the lawn of the residence, but a closer inspection will reveal the tire tracks. There is also a rectangular white highway sign at the beginning of the trail that states "24,000 Pounds Legal Load Limit." This turnoff is just past a cement bridge on VT 12A and just before you reach Braintree's Upper Branch School.

Begin a climb of nearly 3 miles, parts of which may not be rideable because of the grade and condition of the roadbed.

Dunham Brook cascades down the mountain on your left near the road as you begin the ascent. The forest here is composed of relatively new growth, indicating that it may have been open farmland as recently as twenty-five or thirty years ago. At this lower elevation you'll find nice stands of young beech trees. Higher up is a good concentration of birch and, eventually, of maple.

Although seldom used today, this trail was at one time an

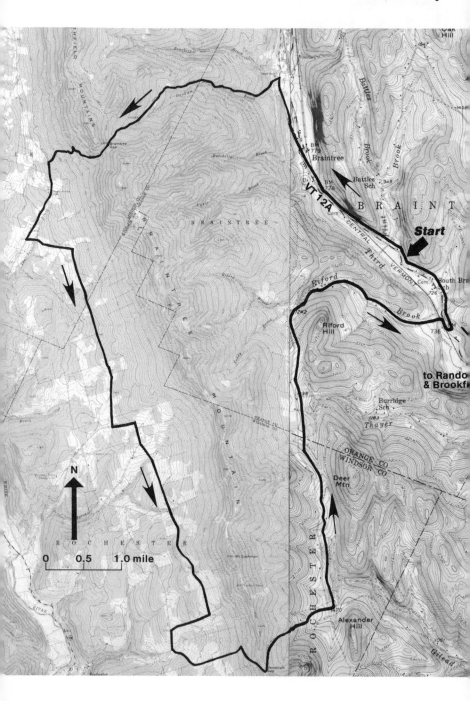

important link to the settlement of Granville on the other side of the mountain. First used near the beginning of the nineteenth century, it provided a way for Granville farmers to reach the Braintree market to buy and sell goods. Later it became a stage route over which passengers and mail were carried to connect with the train.

A Braintree man became lost in the woods while traveling this trail in the early 1800s and was found nine days later with the aid of a dog and a large search party. Local history has it that, upon being found, he was too weak to stand, and he asked first for a drink of water and, then, for some tobacco.

3.3   Turn RIGHT at the fork in the road.

4.7   At a large clearing in the forest, you reach a brown shingled hunting camp on the right. Across from the camp are the remains of a foundation from a building long since gone. Although the terrain appears to level off at this point, the top is yet to be reached.

5.8   Keep to the LEFT at the fork.

5.9   This is the height of land, at 2,390 feet, with the descent beginning just ahead. The trip down the other side is steep in places and rocky throughout, and caution must be observed. Lower your bike's seat and your center of gravity, test the brakes, and remove your feet from toe clips if you use them.

7.0   Turn LEFT onto a maintained dirt road, passing on the right a small seasonal building named "Camp Carp" as you make the turn.

7.1   Pass a private road to the left.

7.4   Pass a cemetery on the left.

7.7   Continue STRAIGHT past a road to the right.

8.1   Turn LEFT at this intersection onto the road that heads downhill.

8.3   Pass the Wild Apple Farm, where you will see some sheep and possibly some turkeys.

8.7   Bear RIGHT around the corner where a road marked by a "Dead End" highway sign comes in on the left.

10.2 Continue STRAIGHT past a road on the right.

11.1 Turn LEFT at this intersection, where there is a breathtaking view — a classic Vermont farm scene in the foreground against a majestic mountain range backdrop.

12.6 Pass the North Hollow Farm on your left.

This farm is unique in that it raises organic poultry, chicken, and pork. The farm sells directly to consumers.

12.7 Keep to the LEFT, past a road running downhill to the right.

14.4 Pass the Mountain Meadow Farm and its extensive trophy collection of deer antlers and ruffed grouse tail feathers mounted on the front of the shed next to the barn.

14.8 Turn LEFT onto the pavement at this intersection, and prepare to take your first left after a brief downhill run.

15.0 Turn LEFT onto a dirt road just past an abandoned house, and begin a half-mile climb.

15.5 At this point, the dirt road gives way to a trail, just past a white house on the right with a mobile home across the road. This is the beginning of the climb to the top of Mount Cushman.

15.8 Turn LEFT at the fork in the road.

16.2 Turn RIGHT at the fork.

16.6 At the top of the climb at "Randolph Gap," take the trail to the RIGHT that heads steeply downhill. This descent is rocky and steep and requires a great deal of caution. Partway down, a series of waterbars installed at intervals to aid water runoff create two- to three-foot moguls that require particular concentration. At least one rider has been tossed over the handlebars while taking these moguls too fast.

This trail was used as a transportation route before 1815, connecting the villages of Randolph and Rochester. It was even used on one occasion around the turn of this century by an entire circus. Elephants were used to pull the heavy wagons up one side and then were used as "brakes" to hold back the wagons during the descent.

For some years after 1879, the trail was used for access to the top of Mount Cushman. Although now overgrown with brambles and littered with dead and dying trees (a grim reminder of the effects of acid rain on our forests), Mount Cushman was once one of the most popular recreation spots around for parties, picnics, dances, and oyster suppers.

Early photographs show a mountaintop cleared of trees, with magnificent views of nearly one hundred miles in several directions. A large fifteen hundred-square-foot building complete with tables, benches, and kitchen facilities was erected at the top, and, according to local history, at the dedication ceremony in 1879 more than one thousand people traveled up this very trail in 229 carriages pulled by 269 horses and two oxen.

By 1936 the area had fallen into disrepair, and a short-lived

Curious Holsteins gather to inspect the mountain bike of a passerby near Rochester.

effort to restore it was undertaken. Nearly six hundred local residents attended that ceremony, traveling to the top in the high-chassis automobiles of that era.

17.6   The trail emerges from the woods and becomes a dirt road. Behind dense vegetation to the left is an old cellar hole.

18.1   Turn LEFT at this four-way intersection. This is the Rochester Hollow Road. It will eventually become the Riford Brook Road, and it carries you much of the final distance back toward the starting point. Continue on this road for the next 6.5 miles.

20.9   Continue STRAIGHT past the Thayer Brook Road on the right. The next 4 miles drop gradually downhill through an increasingly settled area toward VT 12A.

22.1   Continue STRAIGHT past a couple of private roads that appear in quick succession on the right.

24.7   Turn LEFT onto VT 12A and proceed for a little more than a mile back to your vehicle.

26.0   Arrive back at your starting point.

Accommodations
Three Stallion Inn, RD 2, Stock Farm Rd., Randolph, VT 05060 (802-728-5575).
   Lovely Vermont country inn. Beautifully appointed rooms, expertly prepared meals, pool, sauna, tennis, and golf nearby.
Green Trails Country Inn, Brookfield, VT 05036 (802-276-3412).
   Fine dining rooms decorated with antiques and quilts. Swimming, boating, fishing in nearby lake.

Camping
Lake Champagne Campground, Randolph Center, VT 05061 (802-728-3456).
   130 sites; showers, rec hall, swimming, laundry.
Allis State Park, Brookfield, VT 05036.
   Picnic tables and fireplaces, tent sites, lean-tos, trailer sites, and hot showers.

Bicycle Service
Bicycle Express, Depot Square, Northfield, VT (fifteen miles from starting point) (802-485-7430). Sales, service.
Green Mountain Bicycle Service, P.O. Box 253, Route 100, Rochester, VT (fifteen miles from starting point) (802-767-4464). Sales, service, rentals, tours.
Mad River Bike Shop, Rt. 100, P.O. Box 871, Waitsfield, VT (802-496-9500).
New England Bicycle Tours, 41 S. Main Street, Randolph, VT (five miles from starting point) (802-728-3261). Rentals, tours.

Braintree Hill

Distance: 23.0 miles
Difficulty: Strenuous
Riding surface: Mostly gravel, considerable forest trail, some pavement
Towns included: Randolph, Braintree, Brookfield, Roxbury
Maps: USGS 15' Randolph, Barre

Braintree Hill is a fifteen hundred-foot ridge running north to south and paralleling the Braintree Mountain Range to the west. Much of the trip offers spectacular scenery, from picturesque views of the half-dozen working farms along the route to sixty-mile vistas at the summit. The area through which this route passes is rich with wildlife. Sightings of many birds and animals including coyotes, deer, and wild turkeys are not uncommon.

Begin this trip in the village of Randolph, a bustling, self-contained town of four thousand that serves as the commercial center for more than twenty thousand residents of smaller surrounding towns. Situated in the geographic center of the state, Randolph was an early choice for the state capital but was beat out by Montpelier. Today, the town's largest employer is Vermont Castings, the nation's largest manufacturer of cast-iron woodburning stoves. The company's showroom is located on Prince Street next to the river.

Ample parking at the start of the bike route is available in a lot behind the Grand Union supermarket, adjacent to the town office building. The actual departure point for the trip is the Union Market on Main Street, a good place to stock up on sandwiches and picnic supplies. Baked goods can be purchased at The Lost Mountain Book & Bake Shop, just a few doors up Main Street.

0.0 Beginning at the Union Market, proceed north along Main Street and cross the cement bridge spanning the White River.

0.2   Bear RIGHT at the intersection of VT 12 and VT 12A, passing the Cumberland Farms store on the right and the fire station on the left.

0.3   At the intersection of VT 12 and VT 66, marked by the town's only stop light, turn LEFT up Elm Street, a steep but short climb. It is advisable to gear down in advance of this sometimes busy intersection to anticipate the hill. Continue straight.

After a half mile, the residential section gives way to peaceful fields on the right that turn a brilliant yellow when the alfalfa blossoms in early summer. Ayer's Brook meanders south through the fields, and about two miles upstream there is good fishing for brook, rainbow, and brown trout. The stream's namesake, according to local history, was a hapless soldier who deserted the English to become a guide for their enemies during the French and Indian War. He was caught and hanged near the stream about 1755.

1.9   At the fork, bear RIGHT. The pavement ends here.

3.4   At the intersection, turn LEFT onto Peth Road.

The genesis of the unusual moniker "Peth" is uncertain, but it likely is a derivative of the word "pith," meaning center. The one-time bustling village of Peth was the center of the town of Braintree. Like many original Vermont settlements, Peth flourished and prospered in its early years only to suffer eventual commercial decline. The unassuming stream over which the road passes powered a variety of mills, including a wool carding mill, a cider mill, and a sawmill. Other businesses that turned Peth into a modest commercial center were a cabinet shop where wagons and sleighs were made, a blacksmith shop, a clothier's shop, a furniture manufacturer, and a dry goods store. A church and eventually a post office rounded out the community. All that remains of the dreams of Peth's founders are the houses still standing along this quiet lane and the stone foundations of the old mills along the banks of the stream.

3.5   At the Y, bear RIGHT onto Brainstorm Road.

5.7   At the intersection, turn LEFT onto Farnsworth Brook Road, then bear LEFT again almost immediately.

6.2   Turn RIGHT onto Davis Road. In about a mile, just past the first farmhouse you come to on your right, begin an extremely steep and bumpy descent that requires caution.

7.5   Turn LEFT onto Cram Hill Road.

This road very quickly becomes impassible for vehicles but well suited to a mountain bike. For the next mile, the trail becomes increasingly primitive. This trail was frequently traveled in the last century, and evidence of settlement along the trail still exists in stone walls, old cellar holes, and plantings of apple trees and lilacs.

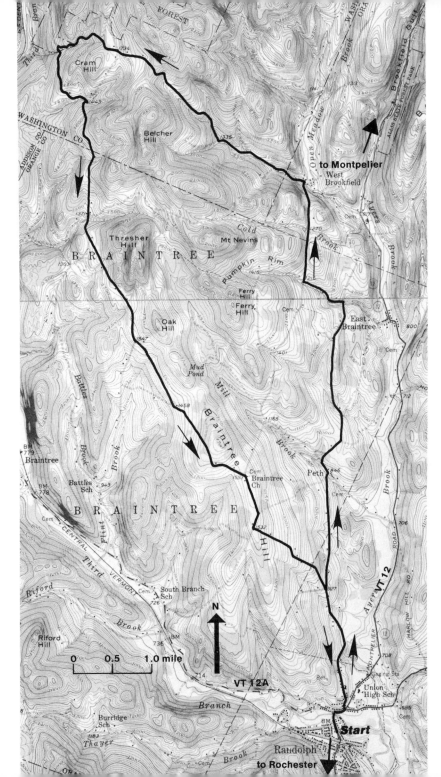

FOREST

Third Branch

Cram Hill
1734
1449

WASHINGTON CO.

Belcher Hill
1335

ADDISON CO.
ORANGE CO.

BRAINTREE

Thresher Hill
1371
1393

Mt Nevins

1500

Pumpkin Rim

Cold

Brook

1270

Brook

to Montpelier

West Brookfield

Brookfield Gulf

WASH. ORA.

1313

1800

1600

ALLIS STATE FOREST PARK

Aurs

Cem

Brook

Ferry Hill
Ferry Hill

Oak Hill
1547

1415

Cem

1401

East Braintree
800

Cem

712

Mud Pond

Mill

1458

1165

Brook

Peth
846

Cem

Battles

Brook

Brook

Brook

BM 779
Braintree

BM 778

Battles Sch
943

Cem Braintree Ch
550

Braintree

1532

Hill

706

BRAINTREE

Cem

CENTRAL

Flint

Brook

VERMONT

Third

South Branch Sch
726

527

Ave VT 12

MONTPELIER

ROAD

HARLOW HILL RD

Riford Brook

N

0   0.5   1.0 mile

Riford Hill

736   BM

708

Brook

714

VT 12A

585

Res.

Union High Sch

Burridge Sch
483

MONTPELIER

Staging Sta

Branch

BM

Start

Cem

Thayer

1283

Brook

Randolph
to Rochester

Low gearing and fat, knobby tires enable the mountain bike to penetrate Vermont's roughest byways.

8.3 Bear LEFT at the fork.

8.9 Continue STRAIGHT past a wooden bridge and trail on the left.

9.1 Continue on the trail as it bends to the right.

9.8 Keep to the LEFT past a trail on the right.

10.1 Here the trail leaves the woods and intersects with a dirt road that is better maintained. Turn LEFT, heading downhill. Pass first a camp on the left and then a house on the right.

10.7 Continue STRAIGHT through what looks like a four-way intersection.
Just ahead you'll pass a trailer on the right surrounded by abandoned automobiles and miscellaneous junk. There may be dogs here that will want to chase you. The best strategy is to pass as quickly and quietly as possible, with your dog repellant handy just in case.

11.5 Turn LEFT at the intersection.

12.6 Turn RIGHT, and take a rest if you need it. The next half mile is a steep climb on loose roadbed that can be difficult to navigate.

13.5 At this point you pass the Maple Ridge Sheep Farm.
Linda and Tut Doane have one of the largest sheep operations in the area with about 120 ewes and 30 of the friendliest rams you'll ever meet, some with magnificent horns. The Doanes specialize in raising natural-colored handspinners fleeces in a multitude of shades from white through gray to jet black, and from light tan to the dark brown color of a chocolate bar. To accomplish this variety, they have sheep from many breeds, including unusual ones such as Red Karakul and over one hundred Shetlands. Their Shetland sheep flock is the first such flock in the United States and the second, outside of Great Britain, in the entire world.

In addition to fleeces and breeding stock, the Doanes sell pelts and commercially spun yarn in an exciting range of natural colors. If you contact them ahead of time at 802-728-3081, you may be able to arrange a tour of the farm to see the sheep and some of their innovative management practices, and perhaps even a wool spinning demonstration.

Raising sheep was the principle agricultural activity in Vermont until its decline around 1850. Interest in sheep farming has enjoyed a revival in Vermont in recent years, and many observers of the trend feel it could become a viable diversification for beleaguered Vermont dairy farms.

14.0 Pass on your left the Connecticut Corners schoolhouse, built in 1820.

14.8 Turn LEFT, passing on your right a private pond and a side road.

15.3   Follow this hairpin turn around to the right. Continue straight on this road
for almost 4 miles, all the way to the Braintree Hill Meetinghouse.

This stretch offers impressive views of the Braintree Range to the
west, a collection of peaks of nearly twenty-five hundred feet.

19.0   Turn RIGHT at the fork.

On your left is the Braintree Meetinghouse, built in 1807 and used
now as the headquarters for the Braintree Historical Society. Because of the spectacular setting, it is used occasionally for weddings
and other special events. This is a good place to pause before the
final leg of the journey, a long, exhilarating descent back into Randolph Village.

The Meetinghouse grounds include a picnic area and an adjacent cemetery, and views from here are excellent on a clear day. To
the east, Mount Washington and the White Mountains of New
Hampshire can be seen at a distance of fifty to sixty miles. To the
south and southwest respectively you can glimpse Vermont's Mount
Ascutney and Killington Mountain, both at distances of around forty
miles. The connected peaks of the Braintree Mountains lie closer to
the west, providing a visual panorama of nearly 360 degrees. The
view is particularly striking during the foliage season, which generally occurs between the last week in September and the first week or
two of October.

19.7   Turn LEFT at this intersection, across from which are located cable
television antennas.

The corn fields on your right as you begin the ascent are a favorite
winter feeding area of wild turkeys, which can occasionally be
sighted in the summer and fall as well.

Caution: The road ahead is sometimes "washboard" rough,
and care should be exercised when making the descent.

21.0   Continue STRAIGHT through this intersection, where you took the other
road earlier in the trip. The next stretch is a paved descent to the stop
light in town.

22.6   Turn RIGHT at the light.

22.8   Bear LEFT across the bridge, and you are once again on Randolph's
Main Street from which you departed.

23.0   Now you are back at the starting point.

Accommodations

Three Stallion Inn, RD 2, Stock Farm Road, Randolph, VT 05060 (802–
728–5575).

Lovely Vermont country inn. Beautifully appointed rooms, expertly prepared
meals, pool, sauna, tennis, and golf nearby.

Green Trails Country Inn, Brookfield, VT 05036 (802–276–3412).
    Fine dining rooms decorated with antiques and quilts. Swimming, boating, fishing in nearby lake.

Camping
Lake Champagne Campground, Randolph Center, VT 05061 (802–728–3456).
    130 sites; showers, rec hall, swimming, laundry.
Allis State Park, Brookfield, VT 05036.
    Picnic tables and fireplaces, tent sites, lean-tos, trailer sites, and hot showers.

Bicycle Service
Bicycle Express, Depot Square, Northfield, VT (fifteen miles from starting point) (802–485–7430). Sales, service.
Green Mountain Bicycle Service, P.O. Box 253, Route 100, Rochester, VT (fifteen miles from starting point) (802–767–4464). Sales, service, rentals, tours.
New England Bicycle Tours, 41 S. Main Street, Randolph, VT (five miles from starting point) (802–728–3261). Rentals, tours.

Graniteville

Distance: 31.7 miles
Difficulty: Strenuous
Riding surface: Gravel and pavement, with some forest trail
Towns included: Brookfield, Williamstown, Barre
Maps: USGS 15' Barre, East Barre

Although much of this route winds through scenic and isolated country roads, it begins and ends at one of Vermont's most popular tourist attractions. The Rock of Ages Quarry in Barre is industry on a massive scale and can be appreciated best with a personal visit. It also makes a good conclusion to a day of cycling.

Out of an open quarry that covers more than twenty acres and is over three hundred-feet deep, massive granite derricks towering 115 feet above the edge of the quarry lift blocks weighing one hundred tons. To dislodge the blocks, skilled laborers use a combination of pneumatic drills, torches, and explosives, but there was a time when sledgehammers and spikes were the chief tools of the trade.

Once the blocks have been removed, they are transported to a finishing shed where they are shaped, finished, polished, and sometimes inscribed. In addition to use as tombstones, the granite is used for curb stones, as building materials, and for huge press rolls that squeeze out moisture in the manufacturing of paper. Some of the finished pieces require precision accuracy in tolerances as close as one hundred-millionths of an inch.

The visitors' center next to the parking lot from which this trip begins is open seven days a week from May through October, and admission is free. You can also take a free twenty-five-minute train ride to the edge of the quarry. The Craftsmen Center a mile down the road is also worth a visit, where an observation deck enables you to view various phases of the granite finishing process taking place in an area the size of two football fields.

Although quarrying has been carried on here for a hundred years,

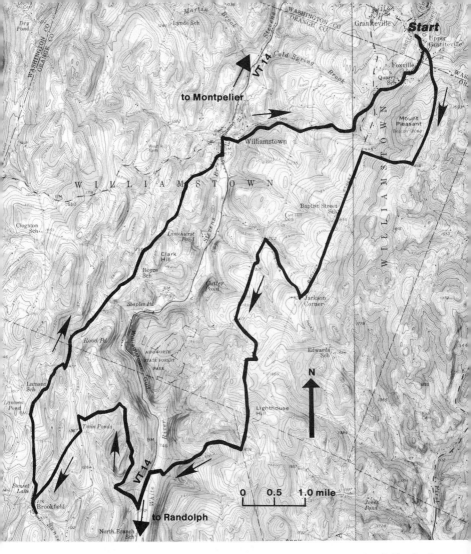

only the surface of the granite deposit has been scratched. Geologists estimate that the granite lode here is about six miles deep, four miles wide, and ten miles long.

0.0 Leave the Rock of Ages parking lot and turn RIGHT.
Although in the town of Barre, this village appropriately is called Graniteville.

0.5 Bear RIGHT at the intersection.

0.7 Go STRAIGHT through this four-way intersection, at which the pavement ends, then head uphill toward the telephone tower.

2.3 Turn RIGHT at the four-way intersection.

3.1   Turn LEFT at the four-way intersection, and pass a collection of large structures carrying electrical wires.

6.6   Turn RIGHT onto the pavement at this four-way intersection.

8.0   Turn LEFT onto the gravel road. Watch closely, for the road is nearly hidden until you are well upon it.

8.5   Bear LEFT at the intersection.

9.4   Bear LEFT at the intersection marked by a sign pointing to "Brookfield" and "East Hill."

10.1 Turn RIGHT at the intersection. In a short distance, the road passes in front of an old farmhouse and becomes a forest trail, with the latter portion of the trail becoming very rough as it goes over ledge.

11.8 Having just left the forest trail, you are once again on gravel and will turn RIGHT at this intersection. These trails are used extensively by snowmobiles in the winter, and a collection of signs maintained by the snowmobile association may be found here. For the next 2 miles the road makes an extremely steep descent.

13.8 Turn LEFT onto VT 14.

14.3 Turn RIGHT onto gravel road, and climb for about a mile. Continue on this road.

16.6 Two small ponds called the Twin Ponds lie down in the valley to your left.

18.0 Turn LEFT.

18.2 Turn RIGHT.

19.8 You have reached Brookfield's Pond Village, home of Vermont's only floating bridge. There is a general store in the village where you can buy refreshments.

The unique floating bridge is one of two such bridges in the United States. Although the current version was built in 1978 by the Vermont Department of Transportation, six other such structures have successively bridged this spot for more than 175 years. The first bridge was built in 1812 after a local man fell through thin ice and drowned. Although varying somewhat in materials and design, all seven bridges have used the same principle: wooden planks strung together and floating freely on buoyant pontoons. Originally the pontoons were probably oak barrels sealed with tar, but the current bridge employs plastic flotation units.

The lake was originally called Colt's Pond, after an early settler by that name, and was later referred to as Mirror Pond. The preferred name is now Sunset Lake. Covering about twenty-five acres and thirty-feet deep in the middle, the lake is a favorite haunt for

Swimmers, fishermen, and curiosity seekers frequent Vermont's only floating bridge throughout the summer.

anglers who try for rainbow trout, perch, pickerel, and bass from the bridge or from canoes. The ragged collection of broken lines and bobbers suspended from the utility line that crosses the pond overhead — casualties of errant casts — will attest to the bridge's popularity as a fishing spot. Hot summer days will also find swimmers diving off the bridge, and if you're doing this trip on such a day you may wish to join them.

Brookfield was also the site of the first circulating library in the state. Established in 1791 to "promote useful knowledge and piety," the initial library included forty books for the town's four hundred residents.

Leave Pond Village heading NORTH, passing the Green Trails Inn on your right as you leave. The inn frequently is an overnight stay for riders on one of the several commercial bicycling tours that operate in Vermont.

20.8 Bear RIGHT at the intersection.

21.3 Turn RIGHT onto the dirt road.

22.3 Turn RIGHT onto the dirt road, then turn immediately LEFT.

22.8 Pass Rood Pond on the right.
This pretty pond attracts anglers throughout the summer as much for its peaceful beauty as for the chance of catching brook trout.

24.8 Bear RIGHT at the fork in the road.

26.9 Turn LEFT onto VT 14 and pass through the village of Williamstown.
Williamstown is the birthplace of Thomas Davenport in 1802. Davenport was born into a large, poverty-stricken family. After serving an apprenticeship to a blacksmith, he moved across the state to Forestdale. There he invented the first electric motor and created a model for the first electric car. He couldn't have done it without the support of his wife, however, since she allowed him to use silk from her wedding dress to wind the essential horseshoe magnet. Davenport died nearly as poor and unrecognized as he had been when he was born, after a lifetime devoted to science.

27.2 Turn RIGHT onto the Graniteville/Websterville Road. Remain on this road with a double-solid middle line for the next 4 miles to Graniteville where this trip began.

31.3 Turn LEFT.

31.7 You have arrived back at the Rock of Ages parking lot.

Accommodations
Three Stallion Inn, RD 2, Stock Farm Road, Randolph, VT 05060 (802–728–5575).
Lovely Vermont country inn. Beautifully appointed rooms, expertly prepared meals, pool, sauna, tennis, and golf nearby.
Green Trails Country Inn, Brookfield, VT 05036 (802–276–3412).
Fine dining rooms decorated with antiques and quilts. Swimming, boating, fishing in nearby lake.

Camping
Lake Champagne Campground, Randolph Center, VT 05061 (802–728–3456).
130 sites; showers, rec hall, swimming, laundry.
Allis State Park, Brookfield, VT 05036
Picnic tables and fireplaces, tent sites, lean-tos, trailer sites, and hot showers.

Bicycle Service
Bicycle Express, Depot Square, Northfield, VT (twelve miles from starting point) (802–485–7430). Sales, service.
Demers Repair, Inc., 81 S. Main St., Barre, VT (802–476–7712).
Onion River Sports, 20 Langdon Street, Montpelier, VT (twenty-five miles from starting point) (802–229–9409). Sales, service.

The Northeast Kingdom

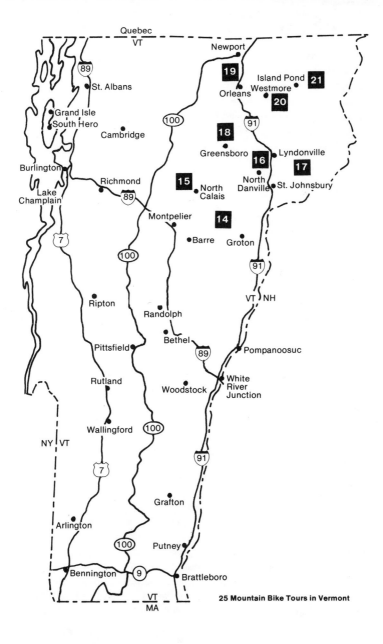

25 Mountain Bike Tours in Vermont

Groton State Forest

Distance: Two trips: 18.9 miles or 12 miles
Difficulty: Moderate/Easy
Riding surface: Smooth, packed gravel (mostly)
Towns included: Groton, Peacham, Marshfield
Maps: USGS 15' Plainfield, East Barre, St. Johnsbury, Woodsville (NH)

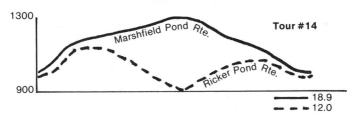

Groton State Forest is a beautiful, rugged area of about twenty-five thousand acres in the lower part of the Northeast Kingdom section of Vermont. Artifacts have been discovered indicating an Indian presence in the Groton wilderness before the seventeenth century. The first white visitors to the area are believed to have been captives of the Deerfield, Massachusetts, Indian raid of 1677, forced to travel through here enroute to Canada.

Because the land is steep, rough, and frequently poorly drained, it was not developed as a farming area. Rather, extensive logging was carried out here beginning in the 1870s, until all the timber was cut about fifty years later. Numerous logging camps operated in the forest, and the abundant water power supported several mills. Getting the lumber to market on a large scale was made possible by the Montpelier—Wells River Railroad, which ran straight through the forest. The railroad was carved through wilderness previously unbroken by mass transportation routes, thus providing the first wide-scale public access to Lake Groton and Ricker Pond. The area quickly became a popular spot for the summer sports—swimming, boating, fishing, and hiking—and for winter day trips for ice skating and snowshoeing. The train operated from 1873 to 1956 and at its peak ran eight passenger trains a day plus additional freight runs.

A forest fire swept through Groton in April of 1883, the worst ever recorded in Vermont. Flames licking one hundred feet into the air traveled two miles and consumed two thousand acres in just half an hour. Residents of the area escaped only by climbing on logs floating on the lakes. Although no one died, property loss was catastrophic: a steam mill with a capacity of twenty thousand feet of lumber a day, two large boarding houses, warehouses, a store, the school, the blacksmith shop, a depot, many homes, twenty-two railroad cars filled with lumber, two million feet of hardwood, and over five hundred cords of hardwood cut to fuel the steam engines. The frontier spirit prevailed, however, and the community quickly rebuilt and resumed commercial logging.

The forest mix in this area was changed abruptly by another severe forest fire that raged through the spruce, fir, and pine in 1903. Replacing that growth was the red maple and yellow and white birch that exist today. During the 1930s, crews working for the Civilian Conservation Corps replanted extensive tracts of spruce and pine. They also built some of the roads and buildings that are now a part of the park.

Today, Groton State Forest supports a wide variety of wildlife including moose, deer, black bear, ruffed grouse, mink, beaver, otter, fisher cats, and loons. It is an excellent base for active vacationers, with numerous hiking and canoeing opportunities in addition to fine mountain biking. The fishing is good, there are canoe rentals and a public swimming beach, and there are nature trails and an excellent nature center as well.

Although the whistle of the old Montpelier—Wells River Railroad blew its farewell salute years ago and the tracks have been dismantled, the original railroad bed has been preserved and kept in good condition. Used as a snowmobile and cross-country ski trail in the winter, the railroad bed makes an excellent mountain bike trail. The surface is sound, the inclines are gentle, there are long straight stretches, and the corners are gradual (as they must be to meet the requirements of a train).

Two trips are documented here, both on sections of the railroad bed. These are excellent trips for children or beginners, not only because of the terrain but because they are out-and-back trips that can be terminated at any point. They are ideal for the more experienced rider as well, because there are numerous side spurs that lead off into the forest, offering more challenging riding and awaiting exploration.

The longer of the routes is the Marshfield Pond trip, named for the body of water by which it passes. It is 18.9 miles. The Ricker Pond trip is 12 miles.

Marshfield Pond Trip

0.0 Begin in front of the Stillwater Campground, with both the access road and the campground registration building on your left.

Although the grade on the rest of this trip is gentle, the first half mile is an arduous climb. If you're riding with children without the stamina for steep climbs or with anyone who dislikes hills, they will enjoy the trip more if they can begin at the half-mile point.

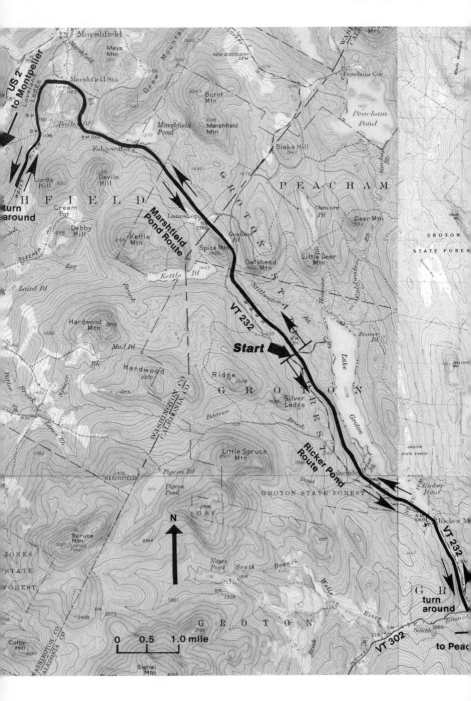

0.5 Turn RIGHT onto the gravel road that is the old railroad bed.

1.3 The road emerges into a clearing that looks as though it is sometimes used as a shooting range.

1.6 To your right is the first of several glimpses you will get of Owl's Head Mountain.
> The views from the top of Owl's Head, elevation 1,956 feet, are spectacular and make it well worth a visit. The trail to the top includes stone steps built by the CCC in the 1930s, and a unique six-sided stone gazebo is located at the top. There is a vehicle access road that takes you to within a tenth of a mile of the top, but the surface is loose gravel in places and the road is very steep, making it undesirable for mountain bikes. Unless you are interested in a particularly demanding challenge, visit Owl's Head later by automobile rather than launch an assault by bike.

2.1 Cross a wooden bridge over a deep but narrow gully down which runs Stillwater Brook.

2.4 Here is the intersection of VT 232. Cross it and pick up the trail on the other side.

2.6 To the right is a good view of Drew Mountain.
> At the same time the view appears, the road dips and the surface deteriorates considerably. Be careful that the view does not distract your attention from this potentially dangerous spot.

3.2 Continue STRAIGHT through this intersection, with a dilapidated barn, a garage, and a couple houses on the hill behind on the left. There may be a dog patrolling this area, but since the road ahead is straight and flat, you can accelerate quickly.

4.0 Continue STRAIGHT past a road leading off to the right.

4.7 Marshfield Pond appears through the trees to your right, as do several private camps.

5.2 There is a turnoff here at the end of Marshfield Pond that offers a picturesque view of the length of the pond and the steep rocky cliff rising above.
> Evidence that a beaver colony has been at work on this end of the pond is clear, as there are two large piles of brush on the embankment that serves as a dam. Also visible are the efforts of man to reinforce the dam. Several large blocks of granite, some showing quarry drill marks, are placed along the dam at intervals.
> The trip beyond here brings a net loss of elevation, resulting in a gradual climb on the return. While most adults will manage the trip

without problem, those with younger children may want to consider turning around here.

5.5   Another pond appears on the right, again showing evidence of beavers at work.

5.6   Turn LEFT at this fork in the road.

6.0   Pass a camp on the left.

6.8   Continue STRAIGHT through this four-way intersection.

7.2   A deep valley drops away on your right, and the sounds of distant traffic on US 2 may be heard.

8.2   A trail leads up into the woods on the left. Close by the road is a shack whose interior has been gutted by fire.

9.4   This large clearing in the forest is the site of a recent logging operation and is the turn-around point of the trip.
           The railroad bed continues for some distance past this clearing, allowing you to explore additional "uncharted territory" if you desire a longer trip. Otherwise, reverse your direction and retrace your route back for 9 miles.

18.4   Turn LEFT onto the pavement from which you departed earlier and make the fast descent back to the starting point. This road may have considerable traffic, particularly during the summer vacation season, and care should be exercised.

18.9   You are now back at the starting point.

Ricker Pond Trip

Because the turn-around point of this trip is a popular local diner named the Green Mountain Restaurant and General Store, you might want to plan your arrival to coincide with mealtime.

0.0   Begin in front of the Stillwater Campground as with the previous trip, with the access road and the campground registration building on your left. Once again, although the grade experienced on the rest of this trip is gentle throughout, the first half mile is an arduous climb. Kids and adults who dislike hills may prefer to avoid this initial climb and begin the trip at the half-mile point.

0.5   Turn LEFT onto the gravel road that is the old railroad bed.

1.0   The land opens up on both sides, the result of recent logging. Already the land is reverting to forest as the more aggressive and fast-growing tree species, like birch and poplar, take hold. In the valley below to your left, long and narrow Lake Groton parallels the road.

2.7   Cross through this four-way intersection and continue STRAIGHT.

3.2   If there is a metal gate across the road, go around it. Just 200 feet ahead, continue STRAIGHT past a road going to the left.

3.3   Continue STRAIGHT through this Y-shaped intersection, passing a park ranger's station on the right and a road running downhill to the left.

3.6   Ricker Pond appears on the left, as well as the state park facilities along the shore.

3.9   Go around the gate if it is across the road.

4.1   Here you reach paved VT 232, and the trail you have been riding on seems to disappear. Actually, it merges briefly with the pavement and re-enters the woods on the other side. Turn left on VT 232 and watch for the trail entering the woods on the right.
   On the left at this point is Ricker's Mills, established in 1790 and operated until1953. The foundation of the most recent mill is still prominent below the new dam on the south end of Ricker Pond. The location of the mill was ideal; not only could logs from the surrounding hills be floated here, but the mill was able to use the same water that had transported the logs to drive its machinery.

4.2   Turn RIGHT onto the trail going into the woods.

4.9   Pass a pig pen on the right, and continue straight past a residence on the right.
   Young pigs are suspicious of strangers. These will invariably fly in panic to the top of the hill, grunting with alarm, and there stand to view you nearsightedly with distrust.

5.6   Continue STRAIGHT past the snowmobile trail leading down to the left.

5.7   Turn LEFT as the trail emerges from the forest to visit the Green Mountain General Store and Restaurant (within view to the left). US 302 is directly in front of you.

5.9   This is the Green Mountain General Store and Restaurant and the turn-around point of the trip. Reverse your route to return to the starting point.

11.5   Turn LEFT onto the paved road, and descend back to the beginning point.

12.0   You are back at the beginning in front of Stillwater Campground.

Accommodations

The Peacham Inn, P.O. Box 93, State Road 1, Peacham, VT 05862 (802–592-3208).
   Built in 1805 in the center of a well-preserved historic village, this peaceful

Young mountain bikers enjoy Vermont's countless opportunities for a picnic or a quick swim.

country inn is close to the Groton State Forest. A continental breakfast is included in the room rate, and rooms with fireplaces and views are available. The meals are prepared with freshness and imagination.

Camping
Groton State Forest, Groton, VT 05046.
   Picnicking, fishing, hunting, hiking, tent sites, trailer sites, hot showers, nature trail, nature center.

Bicycle Service

Bicycle Express, Depot Square, Northfield, VT (802-485-7430).
Demers Repair, Inc., 81 S. Main Street, Barre, VT (802-476-7712).
Onion River Sports, 20 Langdon Street, Montpelier, VT (approximately twenty-five miles from start of tour) (802-229-9409). Sales and service.
Park Pedals, South Walden Road, Cabot, VT (approximately fifteen miles from start of tour) (802-563-2252). Sales and service.

Kent Corners

Distance: 18.4 miles
Difficulty: Moderate
Riding surface: Gravel
Towns included: Calais, Woodbury
Map: USGS 15' Plainfield

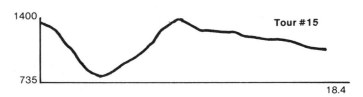

Although the starting point is just eleven miles from Montpelier, Vermont's capital, this trip winds through some old Vermont countryside that quickly evokes a feeling of the past. It is also a trip through one of the "wettest" sections of Vermont: The two towns through which it passes collectively have more standing bodies of water than any other area in the state—forty-one ponds and lakes, all within ten miles of each other. Twenty-five are in the town of Woodbury, fourteen in Calais, and two are shared on the boundary. You will pass five of them.

The land in Calais began being cleared in 1787, prior to settlement, by Francis Chase. Mr. Chase returned to Massachusetts that same year, married, and then walked the 275 miles back to Calais with his new bride. Just for the record, the residents of Calais disregard the French origin of the name. They pronounce it in a practical and no-nonsense fashion, as "Callous."

The Kent Tavern Museum at which this journey begins was built in 1837 using bricks and iron made in the town and lumber sawed down the road. More a country inn and stagecoach stop than a tavern, the building was operated for nine years as a hotel, but marriage compelled owner Abdiel Kent to convert it for use as his family home in 1846. Typical of such lodging places, it was equipped with an upstairs ballroom in addition to a tap room and guest rooms.

The Kent family sold the property in 1916, but it was bought back by Atwater Kent (of Atwater Kent Radio fame) in 1930 and restored. He eventually donated it to the Vermont Historical Society, and that group continues to operate it as a museum featuring rural agricultural and

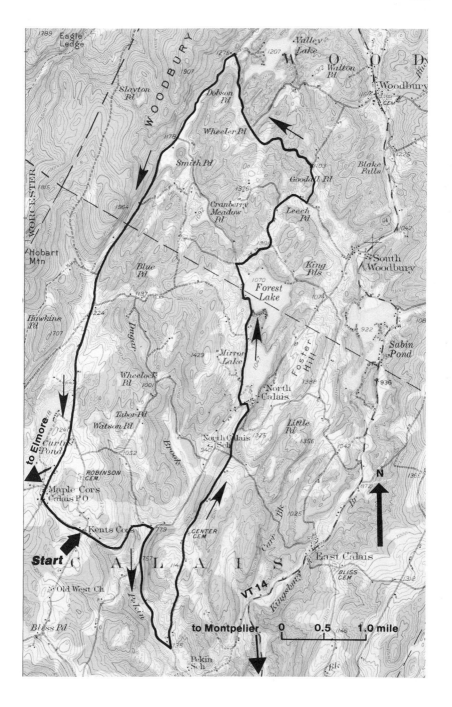

industrial exhibits and workshops. It is generally open on summer after-
noons and fall weekends, but exact hours can be determined by calling
the museum at 802–828–2291.

0.0   Begin this trip with the Kent Museum on your right, and, passing the
stately White House Restaurant on your right as well, head downhill for
just over a mile.

0.5   The Swiss American Traditions Canoe Yard and Woodworking Shop is
on your left.

1.1   At this intersection, just past the Calais town hall, turn RIGHT.
The building you have just passed was constructed in 1825 and
served as the spiritual headquarters of the community for many
years. Although it was used every Sunday, it contained no stove for
the first six years. When January temperatures plunged to near zero
degrees and the arctic winds whipped through the valley, the fires of
hell must have seemed almost inviting.

Religious fervor reached a peak in Calais on the night of De-
cember 31, 1843. On that night, the church was packed with followers of William Miller, who had fifty thousand or so followers
nationwide and who had an enthusiastic representation in Calais.
Miller had used scripture to prophesy that on the last day of that
year the world would end, with the earth and sea giving up their
dead and the saved passing on into eternal bliss. A large wooden
clock was brought in and set near the pulpit, and the nervous souls
in attendance sat and waited for the midnight hour. As it ap-
proached midnight, some screamed, and some fainted. That, however, was the extent of the action. Ten minutes later, the church was
empty and the Millerites homeward bound, sobered by such a close
call but no doubt joyful at the prospect of a second chance.

Another unusual story concerns Pardon Janes, a young man
who was an inspiring Calais civic leader and state legislator in the
early nineteenth century. At some point, Mr. Janes became ob-
sessed with a distrust of people and a fear of germs that grew so
great that he took to strapping a pitchfork to his wrist so he wouldn't
have to touch anyone. Simple transactions such as the exchange of
money were accomplished using a small metal pail that hung from
one of the tines. It is unclear whether it was a particular incident that
touched off the eccentricity, or if it had to do with his experience in
politics.

2.8   Take a rather sharp LEFT at this intersection and prepare for a challenging climb for about a mile. Look for a flock of sheep in the field on your
left as you begin the ascent.

4.1   You'll pass a cemetery on the right.

5.2 Continue STRAIGHT through this four-way intersection.

5.9 Bear LEFT at the fork.

6.0 Turn LEFT at this intersection, then take your first RIGHT just a few hundred feet ahead and climb a short but abrupt hill.
For a short diversion, visit the antique shop in sight just up the hill from this intersection.

6.2 Mirror Lake is on your right.
Lucky anglers catch rainbow and lake trout early in the spring in this eighty-six-acre lake and smallmouth bass later in the summer. On calm days, the surface can imitate the mirror its name implies, but a sudden squall one dark afternoon in the late 1800s capsized a boat containing twenty-three people returning from a picnic, drowning five of them.

7.2 Forest Lake is on your right.
The second of the forty-one ponds and lakes in the area that you pass, this is another favorite of boaters, campers, and fishermen. Forest Lake covers 125 acres and is up to 200-feet deep, and it offers excellent fishing for rainbow and lake trout in addition to bass

7.8 Turn RIGHT at this four-way intersection and begin a challenging ascent for about 1/2 mile, with Forest Lake dropping away into the valley on your right as you climb.

8.3 Bear LEFT at this intersection.

8.7 Pass under the barn access built over the road.

8.9 Bear RIGHT and begin a steep descent.

9.3 Turn LEFT at this intersection.
As you turn the corner you'll see a small body of water off to your right with the uninviting name of Leech Pond.

9.7 Bear LEFT at this intersection, just past an A-frame house on the left.

10.8 Pass Wheeler Pond on the left.

11.1 Pass Dobson Pond on the left.

11.8 Turn LEFT at the intersection, and continue STRAIGHT for the next 6 miles.

17.7 Having reached the small community of Maple Corners, turn LEFT at the intersection and continue STRAIGHT. The road you did not take to the right is paved.

18.4 You are once again at Kent Corners.

Accommodations

North Branch House, 22 North Street, Montpelier, VT 05602 (802–229–0878).
   A ten-minute walk to the capitol building, less by bike. Decorated with
   antiques and quilts made and silk-screened by the owners, the Kitzmillers.

Camping

Elmore State Park, Lake Elmore, VT 05657.
   Picnic tables and fireplaces, swimming, boating, fishing, hiking, tent sites,
   lean-tos, and hot showers.

Bicycle Service

Demers Repair, Inc., 81 S. Main Street, Barre, VT (802–476–7712).

Onion River Sports, 20 Langdon Street, Montpelier, VT (802–229–9409) (approximately ten miles from starting point). Sales and service.

16

North Danville

Distance: 7.1 miles
Difficulty: Easy
Riding surface: Maintained gravel
Towns included: Danville
Map: USGS 7.5' metric St. Johnsbury

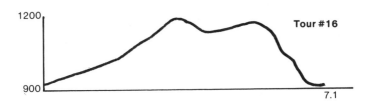

The population of Danville grew from zero to twelve in March of 1784 when the Sias family took up permanent residence as the town's first settlers. It was March, and Captain Charles Sias moved his wife and ten children — the oldest was eleven — plus the family's belongings through deep snow on a hand sled. It took him three trips on three consecutive days. The first thing required of the family upon arrival at the new homestead was to dig out the cabin from the drifted snow so that they could enter. They tapped maple trees almost immediately and enjoyed the sweet sap as a nutritional supplement and springtime treat.

Six years later, two hundred families lived in Danville, and the town had been named for the French Admiral D'anville for reasons no longer remembered. Unfortunately, drought impaired food production in the new community, and they were forced in winter to import corn and other provisions on hand sleds over the many miles of barely passable roads from New Hampshire. Maple sap and sugar continued to be a regular part of their diet.

Long a summertime hideaway for hay fever sufferers, today's Danville is known as the headquarters of the American Society of Dowsers, an organization of twenty-six hundred members in seventeen countries who specialize in finding underground water sources using forked sticks or other instruments of choice.

0.0 Begin the trip in the village of North Danville in front of the North Danville Baptist Church, with the church on your left. Proceed straight ahead, keeping to the LEFT and entering the dirt road as the paved main road

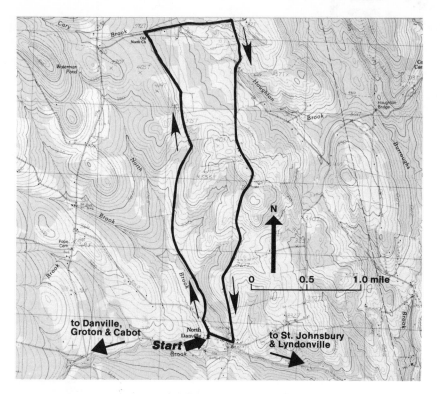

veers away to your right. On the left side of the road, a small, wooden,
three-foot sign for the Old North Church, white with black lettering, marks
the way.

0.2 Turn RIGHT onto the dirt road, passing again a sign for the Old North
Church that points in the direction you are traveling. Dip down, cross a
bridge, and pass first a maple sugaring shack and then a small sawmill
on your left.

What the early settlers would have given for a sawmill to simplify
their building of homes! Like so many other Vermont settlers at the
time, Captain Sias had spent the previous summer building their
cabin, and it was at best rudimentary. First, he selected a suitable
piece of ground and made sure it was near a cold spring of water.
Next, a hole was dug for a crude cellar in which a few bushels of
vegetables could be stored. Stones were laid for a foundation, and
the trunks of suitable-sized trees were cut to proper length, notched
at the extremities, and laid down one upon another. In this way the
walls were built, with space being left for a door. When the walls
became high enough, the logs were cut shorter and shorter, beginning at the eaves, until the last two logs came together at the top to

form the inverted V of the peak. When this framework was completed, the roof was covered with bark from elm trees that had previously been cut in large pieces and dried. Using as fasteners the pieces of the inner bark that twisted like cords, the bark was fastened to small poles that were laid crossways from front to back and tied at the ends. The roof was finished by placing a large piece of bark as a ridge cap astride the ridge pole and securely fastening it as well. Spruce or basswood logs split through the center, smoothed with the ax, and jointed at the edges formed the door. Sod and clay filled the chinks between the logs to keep out drafts.

3.0 Turn RIGHT at this intersection, with the Old North Church, dated 1832, on the right.

Services are still held in the church on Sunday evenings in the summer and fall.

3.8 Turn RIGHT at this intersection with excellent views to the southeast and south, and begin a descent.

Historical accounts of Vermont's past usually include information about the potash industry, the lumber industry, and sheep and dairy farming, but little is said about the booming trade in hard liquor during the early 1800s. Between 1800 and 1820, there was scarcely a town in the state that did not have at least one distillery. Rye, corn, and potatoes were principle ingredients for the distilleries, and apples were used to make cider, which became apple brandy rather than vinegar.

At peak production, there were over two hundred distilleries in the state, and vast quantities were exported for army use as well as civilian consumption. Danville alone had seventeen distilleries, more than any other town in Vermont.

Vermont distilleries concentrated on quantity rather than quality, for they faced stiff competition from Irish or Scotch brands. Eventually British imports secured much of the market, and the price per gallon fell from $1.50 to 33¢ a gallon. Long after the amount exported from Vermont had been reduced to a trickle, an incredible 150 distilleries still remained in the state — apparently to satisfy the home thirst.

In 1817 the state legislature decided to investigate the excessive use of "ardent spirits," and it found that hard liquor was nearly as common as cider. Although there are few reliable measures of actual liquor consumption at that time, one report in 1830 stated that in a single year sixteen thousand gallons of liquor were sold to the three thousand residents of Montpelier; another estimate at the time claims that an average of two gallons was consumed by every man, woman, and child.

4.3 Cross Houghton Brook.

These North Danville horses pause from an afternoon meal to offer a silent greeting to passing cyclists.

4.4 Continue STRAIGHT, passing a road on the left, and shortly after begin a climb.

5.1 Pass a cemetery on the right.

5.3 Pass the Tip Top Dairy Farm, with the barn on your left, and begin another descent.

> Before the railroad came to Vermont in the mid-1800s, commercial travel was done exclusively by stagecoach, a mode of travel not nearly as romantic and charming as it has been made to seem by movies and novels. Ragged mountains, swift streams, and dense forest cover made travel difficult. Existing roads, such as they were, were carved up by wagons loaded with logs. Large sections of roads were washed out in spring floods, and the annual spring "mud season" turned them to quagmires for weeks.
>
> Bumps and bruises were accepted as part of the price stage-coach travelers paid. But more serious accidents were not uncommon, and occasionally someone paid with his life. Descents down the steep mountain trails were among the most dangerous parts of the trip.
>
> Rough-and-tumble drivers, characterized by a fondness for the drink to be found at each stagecoach stop, a willingness to take risks, resourcefulness, and their colorful profanity, drove the teams of up to six horses. When the coach sank to its belly in mud, male passengers were expected to dismount and help free it. And since men wore their best clothes to travel, they were seldom eager to perform the task.

6.9 Here the road turns to pavement and plunges steeply downhill, bending sharply to the right just ahead.

7.0 Turn RIGHT, cross the bridge, and climb a slight grade past a cluster of homes — the center of North Danville.

7.1 Once again you are at the intersection near the North Baptist Church where the trip began.

Accommodations

Broadview Farm, North Danville, VT 05828 (802-748-9902).

> Three miles north of North Danville, this has been a welcome refuge for travelers for more than one hundred years. Single and double accommodations, plus a family apartment. Very reasonable rates.

Sherryland, Danville, VT 05828 (802-684-3354).

> A large old farmhouse dating to the last century, about a mile outside the village in a pleasant country setting. Five homey rooms, no meals, reasonable rates.

Echo Ledge Inn, Route 2, East St. Johnsbury, VT 05838
(802-748-4750).
Danville Inn, Danville, VT 05828 (802-684-3484).
Also a restaurant, located in the center of the village, very pleasant.

Camping
Groton State Forest, Groton, VT 05046.
Picnicking, fishing, hunting, hiking, tent sites, trailer sites, hot showers, nature trail, nature center.

Bicycle Service
Park Pedals, South Walden Road, Cabot, VT (802-563-2252).
St. Jay Hardware, 39 Eastern Avenue, St. Johnsbury, VT (802-748-8076).
Village Sports Shop, US 5, Lyndonville, VT (802-626-8448).

Victory

Distance: 27.2 miles
Difficulty: Strenuous
Riding surface: Primarily maintained gravel, with about 3 miles of forest trail and some connecting pavement
Towns included: Burke, Victory
Map: USGS 15' Burke

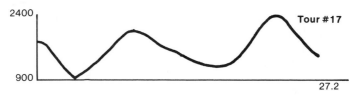

This trip is an expedition through some of the finest wilderness left in Vermont, perhaps in the entire Northeast. Beginning at Burke Mountain, a popular downhill ski area north of St. Johnsbury, this route travels to the tiny settlement of Gallup Mills and then follows the Moose River around the outskirts of Victory bog, an area rich in wildlife, birds, and northern plant species. It then returns to the start over a primitive road built by the Civilian Conservation Corps in 1935.

Thousands of acres in the Burke Mountain area were once owned by Elmer A. Darling, a Burke native who left Vermont to make his fortune as owner of New York's Fifth Avenue Hotel. He returned to buy eight thousand acres of land on the slopes of Burke Mountain, where he raised Morgan horses. Darling donated seventeen hundred acres of his land to the state in 1933, which became the Darling State Forest. The portion where the ski area now operates was subsequently leased to the Burke Mountain Corporation, and it continues under that management.

0.0 Proceed from in front of the Old Cutter Inn, with the inn on your left.

0.5 Begin a steep downhill run around the rim of a valley that drops away to your left, providing good views in that direction.

> Burke may be the only town in Vermont — or anywhere, for that matter — to have had its schoolhouse destroyed by turkeys. The incident happened more than 150 years ago, when "driving the turkeys" to market was an annual fall event in Vermont. These drives went on for nearly seventy years before the railroad and refrigeration offered a reasonable alternative.

Like the cattle drives of the West, turkey drives covered many miles and required a certain amount of expertise. The market was 150 miles away in Boston, and the trip might take two or three weeks. The trek was sufficiently long that the birds' feet were sometimes coated with tar to make an improvised shoe to prevent the foot from wearing out during the trip.

Drives would often include up to four thousand birds from many farms, with one drover for every one hundred turkeys. Bigger drives were occasionally held, with up to ten thousand birds and one hundred drovers. In addition, each drive required several wagons to transport camping supplies and several tons of grain.

Predators were sometimes a problem, and night watches were necessary. One of the least controllable parts of the drive, however, was the roosting instinct that overtook the birds en masse near the end of the day. At that time, the birds would simultaneously fly upward to roost in whatever was available. Since each bird weighed an average of twenty-five pounds, this sudden accumulation of weight could strip trees of their limbs or damage fragile farm buildings and roofs. Such was the case in Burke. Dusk fell just as the flock neared the school, and a thunderous display of beating wings filled the air as the birds jockeyed for position on the school roof. The building creaked under the weight, sagged, and slowly sank in a din of splintering wood and the loud gobbles of several hundred agitated turkeys.

Although the turkey drives may have lacked the rugged romanticism of Western cattle drives, they were a practical and necessary part of the food supply system.

0.9   Begin a climb that is steep but brief — about a quarter mile in length. Once at the top, you'll again enjoy fine views to your left and will start a prolonged descent for more than 2 miles.

3.3   Turn RIGHT onto paved VT 114.

3.7   Turn RIGHT off VT 114 onto gravel road with signs indicating that you have chosen the way to Gallup Mills and Granby. Begin a steep climb on a brief stretch of pavement for about a half mile. Although there is more climbing for the next 4.5 miles, the grades are more gradual.

4.3   The pavement ends, and gravel road begins.

4.8   With the climbing finished for the moment, pass a sign warning that the large swath cut through the wilderness at this point contains both oil and natural gas pipelines. You will crisscross this pipeline several times before the trip is done.

5.4   Continue STRAIGHT past a road on the left.

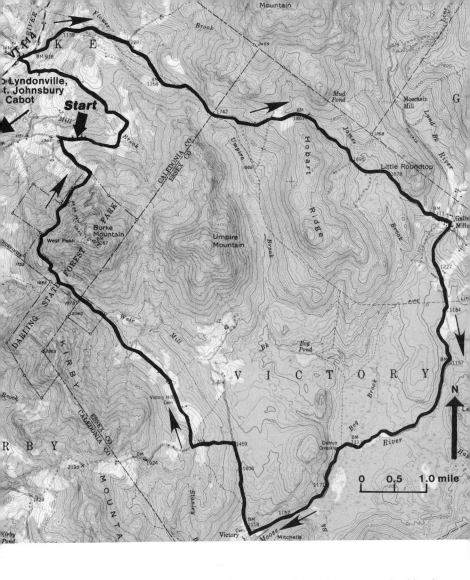

8.4 By this point, you have behind you most of the climbing required by the first half of the trip.

11.1 Here the road turns again to pavement for a very steep but brief descent that leads you to a small settlement of several aged houses intermixed with more recently constructed camps. This small community is Gallup Mills.

Gallup Mills and Victory have a combined population of around 120 people, but it was once a bustling lumbering area. There were several sawmills in the vicinity, hence the name Gallup Mills.

11.7   Turn RIGHT onto a gravel road, passing on your right as you turn a long line of a dozen or more mailboxes.

13.0   Pass the gas pipelines once again, and a quarter mile ahead cross a bridge spanning the Moose River, an attractive stream that follows the road for the next few miles.

14.3   The turnoff on your left is marked by a sign for the Victory Basin Wildlife Management Area.

Ecologists have long viewed the Victory Basin area as an ideal nature preserve, but development pressure from outside interests dates back more than fifty years. In 1936, the Army Corps of Engineers presented a plan to build a dam nine hundred-feet long and ninety-feet wide on the Moose River to provide flood control. When local people pointed out that flooding had not been a problem prior to that point, and that the absorbent nature of the bog provided a form of natural flood control, the plan was put on hold.

Next came a plan that included recreation as well as flood control. Under this plan, the vast lake of nearly a thousand acres would draw tourists to the area and thereby stimulate the region's economy. Local opposition was equally intense, and spokesmen for the community reminded the developers that there were already dozens of beautiful lakes in the Northeast Kingdom and that one more would not likely make a difference. They also pointed out that the massive amounts of vegetation in the bog would make the proposed lake tea-colored and uninviting to swimmers.

For thirty years the bog was left alone. Then, in 1969, the plan for "Vermont Village" was unveiled. This proposal, drawn up by outside developers, called for the establishment of a theme park/ museum that would be the Vermont equivalent of Old Sturbridge Village in Massachusetts. Vermonters would dress up in old-time costumes and display the lifestyle of the past. There would be a large visitors' center, restaurant, and so on. The rationale for the plan was once again to stimulate the local economy. Again, an overwhelming negative reaction to the idea by local folks chased the idea out of town.

The final threat came in the summer of 1988 when the paper company that owned much of the land announced plans to sell off its holdings to a private concern, whose background was largely in the development of mobile home parks. Acting quickly, the state of Vermont entered into negotiations with the paper company and managed to purchase more than seven thousand acres, thereby assuring that the wilderness will be preserved.

16.4   Pass a vehicle parking area on the right.

17.5   Pass another vehicle parking area on the right.

18.5 Turn RIGHT, and begin the final series of climbs for this trip; you will travel nearly 6 miles before you reach the height of land, but not all of this distance is a direct ascent.

19.9 Turn LEFT.

20.6 Continue on the road as it bends to the right, passing a forest road on the left and a weathered residence on the right.

21.5 Pass a cemetery on the left.

21.7 Pass a farm.

21.9 Continue STRAIGHT past a driveway leading up to a house and barn on the left.

22.6 Continue STRAIGHT past a forest road on the left.

22.7 Pass a gravel pit on the left and begin a brief descent.

23.0 Turn LEFT onto a trail that enters the forest. At this same point, the dirt road you have been traveling on bends sharply to the right in a ninety-

Through the morning fog, the view to Lake Willoughby from Burke Mountain.

degree turn. Although unmarked, the trail onto which you will turn is conspicuous and has a cluster of four or five maple trees growing to the left of the entrance, a single maple growing to the right.

For nearly the next 2 miles you will encounter an uphill climb as you cross to the other side of Burke Mountain. Fortunately there are numerous plateaus that break up the climb.

23.9 Keep RIGHT past a snowmobile trail that runs downhill to the left. This intersection is marked by a snowmobile sign nailed to a tree with an arrow pointing to the left.

24.0 Pass a log lean-to on the left. This building is part of the Burke Mountain Campground and is available to campers for a fee.

24.8 This is the height of land, with a descent before you. Take this downhill with caution, for there are fist-sized rocks and chunks of granite that can be treacherous.

At the bottom of the descent, you'll cross three of the main trails that are used by skiers in the winter. The views to the north and the Lake Willoughby area are spectacular.

26.1 Turn LEFT onto the paved Burke Mountain Summit Road and begin a fast descent.

A right turn at this junction would take you to the summit observation platform for a marvelous panorama of much of the terrain covered during this trip — picturesque Lake Willoughby to the north, cradled between the sheer faces of Mounts Hor and Pisgah; wild, continuous forest to the northeast; and the White Mountains to the east. However, the climb is a steep one and is best done by automobile at the conclusion of the trip or by bike on a different day.

26.6 Pass on your right the Sugar Shack, headquarters of the Burke Mountain Campground and where tolls for the summit road are paid. The summit road is a toll road to motor vehicles but free to hikers and bicycles.

26.8 Bear RIGHT past a road on the left that leads to some condominiums.

27.0 Turn RIGHT at the sign for the Old Cutter Inn.

27.1 Continue STRAIGHT past a road on the left.

27.2 You have arrived back at the Old Cutter Inn parking lot.

Accommodations

The Old Cutter Inn, R.R. 1, Box 62, East Burke, VT 05832 (802–626–5152).
Housed in a building constructed in 1845 and located on the Burke Mountain Access Road, the Old Cutter Inn offers quiet, comfortable lodging, an excellent dining room open to the public for dinner six nights a week, a cocktail lounge, and breakfasts available for house guests.

Blue Wax Farm, Pinkham Road, East Burke, VT 05832 (802–626–5542).
An old cape with splendid views of the Lake Willoughby area, comfortable, interesting decor, outside sauna, breakfast.
Echo Ledge Inn, Route 2, East St. Johnsbury, VT 05838 (802–748–4750).

Camping
Burke Mountain Camping, East Burke, VT 05832.
Located on the Burke Mountain Access Road; picnic tables and fireplaces, eighteen tent sites, eight lean-tos, firewood, hot showers.

Bicycle Service
East Burke Sports, Inc., Box 189, Rt. 118, East Burke, VT (802–626–3215).
Gagnon Sports, 25 Railroad Avenue, Orleans, VT (802–754–6466).
Park Pedals, South Walden Road, Cabot, VT (802–563–2252).
St. Jay Hardware, 39 Eastern Avenue, St. Johnsbury, VT (802–748–8076).
Village Sports Shop, US 5, Lyndonville, VT (802–626–8448).

Greensboro

Distance: 26.7 miles
Difficulty: Strenuous
Riding surface: Mostly gravel, some forest trail, some pavement
Towns included: Greensboro, Glover, Craftsbury
Maps: USGS 15' Hardwick, Lyndonville

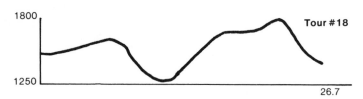

The scenery along this route is some of the finest in Vermont, for the way winds past many well-kept dairy farms, clean pastures interspersed among the mixed hard- and softwood forest, and three beautiful lakes.

The Greensboro area has long been a favorite retreat for the intellectual elite of the East. Writers, musicians, and academics for fifty years or more have found the mix of intellectual stimulation and unsurpassed rural tranquility rejuvenating. Located on the shores of beautiful Caspian Lake, Greensboro was a popular fishing and hunting spot for Indians and later for white settlers from surrounding towns. The first formal visit with an eye to settlement came in 1787 when two preachers camped by the lake and prayed for three days that the area would prosper. A look at the many handsome cedar-shingled camps that line the lake might indicate that the prayers were answered.

In 1788, a winter meeting was held in nearby Cabot by the proprietors of the land, and they agreed to arrange for a permanent settlement to be established at what is now Greensboro. The only dark note on this forward-looking and momentous occasion was that one of the proprietors named Timothy Stanley received severe frostbite damage to a foot on the way to the meeting. For lack of more advanced surgical instruments, he had to have the gangrenous limb removed with a chisel and mallet.

0.0 Begin in the village of Greensboro with The Willey's Store on your right. Leave the village, heading toward the Greensboro Health Center, which you pass on your left. Also pass on your left the United Church of Christ and the Caspian Grange Building.

0.2 Turn RIGHT at the intersection and pass the town clerk's office on the left; just ahead, pass the Greensboro Elementary School on your left.

0.5 The pavement ends, and the road drops.

0.8 Turn RIGHT at the intersection.

2.1 Continue on the main road as it bends to the left, passing on your right a trail entering the woods.

3.0 Turn RIGHT.

3.8 Turn LEFT, drop with a sharp descent into a valley, and climb the other side.

4.8 Continue STRAIGHT past a road on the right and pass the Carroll Shatney and Sons farm.

4.9 Continue STRAIGHT past a road on the left.

5.1 Just past a ranch-style house on the left, the road becomes a trail entering the woods. Continue onto the trail.

5.7 Cross the bridge over Mud Pond Brook, and just ahead pass a seasonal dwelling on the left.

5.9 Keep to the RIGHT past a trail going to the left.

6.1 Continue STRAIGHT past a trail going to the right.

6.9 Turn LEFT onto paved VT 16. Pass by a highway rest area on the right, with a large, flat marshy area to your left. You have now entered the town of Glover and are at the original site of Runaway Pond, where one of the more bizarre events of this area's early history occurred:

It took place in early June of 1810, and residents of the town of Glover found it to be an event that for years afterwards would serve as an example that man had no business tampering with God's handiwork.

That summer was a dry one, and it seemed unlikely that the Barton River that powered the local mills would have enough water flow to last the summer. As a solution, the local men lit upon the idea that they could divert water to the river from nearby Long Pond, a lake more than a mile in length and up to one hundred-feet deep that probably contained more than a billion gallons of water.

Since the lake was only a few hundred feet away, the men were able to dig a channel at the north end of the pond in only a few hours one morning. However, the soil through which the channel was dug was sandy and porous, and the flowing water quickly made the ditch much deeper and wider than the men had intended. Suddenly, with a roar that shook the earth, the entire north bank of the

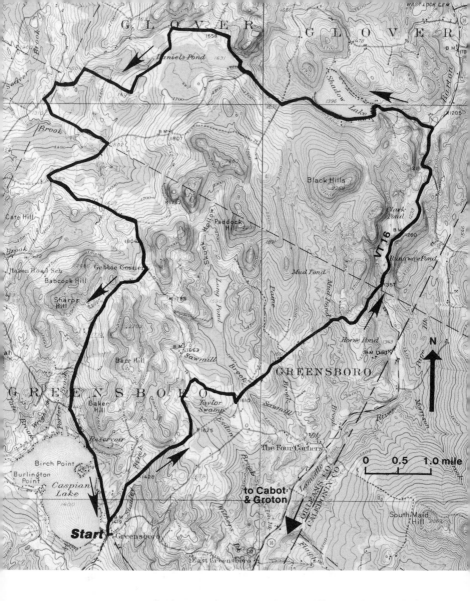

pond—later discovered to have a quicksand-like consistency below ground— collapsed, and the lake began to rush northward. It was a monster out of control, a wall of water that in narrow ravines reached seventy feet in height, was several hundred feet wide, and several miles long. The flood tore through the village of Glover and continued to flow northward, washing away bridges, mills, livestock, and houses built near its banks. When it rushed through the village of Barton twenty-five miles and seven hours later, the high water mark was more than twelve feet above the main street. Shortly after Barton, the flood dispersed into Lake Memphremagog, leaving in its wake several tons of fish that the local folk no doubt collected and preserved. Lake Memphremagog, a twenty-mile-long body of water, is said to have been raised four inches by the massive input of water. Long Pond is now referred to as Runaway Pond, and all that remains of it is the quiet marshy area that you see along the road. A granite marker along the road commemorates the event. If you inspect the soil along the logging road on the north end of the marsh, you'll see its sandy and porous character.

8.0   Pass Tildy's (or Clark's) Pond on your left, famous for its lily pads.

The town of Glover is the home of the Bread and Puppet Theater, a theatrical group that uses huge twenty-foot puppets in skits that celebrate life and often address social problems. The Bread and Puppet group has performed throughout the world, and each summer it holds a two-day puppet festival in an outdoor amphitheater that is attended by ten thousand people or more.

Over the years progress in Glover has always kept pace with the rest of the country, for townspeople acquired all the new major conveniences as they became available: The first cookstove came to town in 1843, making fireplace cooking obsolete. Kerosene lamps were available in 1870, and the first telephones, in 1886. In 1890 a house was constructed with the first built-in bath and toilet. The first car arrived in town in 1908, and the first airplane landed in town in 1941 to deliver a recently caught fish to a local taxidermist for mounting.

Rightfully proud of its accomplishments, perhaps Glover's grandest gesture was her bid to have the Statue of Liberty erected in town when that gift was first offered to the United States by France in the 1880s. Imagine how the destiny of this remote community might have changed had the statue raised her arm over the Vermont forest instead of over New York Harbor.

If all that weren't enough, Glover is perhaps the only small town in New England whose community history has been written in verse, thanks to local poet Harry Alonzo Phillips.

9.5   Turn LEFT onto the road to Shadow Lake and begin a climb of about a mile.

10.5   Shadow Lake appears, and the road winds around the edge of the lake past some camps. As you get toward the far end of the lake, the road begins to climb again.

The outlet of this lake at one time supplied water power to a bustling collection of mills and manufacturing concerns that was coined Slab City, perhaps because of the slab wood that remained after logs had

The devastating power of a billion gallons of water was accidentally unleashed from this spot in Glover in 1810 by well-meaning residents.

been milled. Today, however, Shadow Lake is enjoyed for its recreational potential. Over 188 acres and up to 138-feet deep, the lake contains rainbow, brook, and lake trout and has a public beach. The summer population increases dramatically as a result of the 150 camps built along its shore.

12.3 Turn RIGHT, heading in the same direction as that indicated by the sign for "Rodger's Farm Vacations."

12.8 Pass on your right the red building labeled "Ye Olde Dance Hall."

13.0 Turn RIGHT at the fork, and just ahead reach picturesque Daniel's Pond. Continue on the road as it climbs slightly and winds its way above the pond.

Since there is no other road that provides access to this beautiful pond, the western shore remains essentially undeveloped. The thirty or so camps are clustered on the east end. Somewhat smaller than Shadow Lake at 125 acres, Daniel's Pond offers fishing for largemouth bass, pickerel, and perch. Before electric refrigeration was available, local folks cut ice from this pond every winter. In the spring, the annual sucker run in the outlet brook drew large crowds to watch and capture these migrating fish for food. Today, a colony of beavers resides at Daniel's Pond.

13.9 Continue STRAIGHT past a road on your right.

14.5 Turn LEFT, again going in the direction of the sign for "Rodger's Farm Vacations."

15.1 Pass the Rodger's Farm and be prepared for a boisterous group of dogs. See note under "Accommodations."

15.7 Follow the road as it bends sharply to the RIGHT, away from another trail going to the left.

16.5 Turn LEFT.

17.1 Turn LEFT.

17.4 Turn LEFT.

18.2 Continue STRAIGHT past a private drive leading up to a farm.

18.6 Turn RIGHT.

19.8 Turn LEFT.

19.9 Turn LEFT.

20.9 Pass a dead-end road on the right.

21.0 Pass on the left a cemetery.

21.4   Bend to the RIGHT with the road as it passes a trail entering the forest on the left.

22.1   Turn RIGHT.

22.4   Pass the Maplehurst Farm and climb a hill. Once at the top, you begin a straight, continuous downhill run to Caspian Lake.

23.2   At this point, you get your first glimpse of Caspian Lake.
Deep, cold, and over seven hundred acres in size, there is excellent fishing in the lake for trout and landlocked salmon. Caspian stretches for a mile and a half in length, and is between a half mile and one mile in width.

24.7   At the bottom of the long descent, turn LEFT onto the paved road and make a steep but brief climb to the Highland Lodge Ski Touring Area and Restaurant.

26.5   Pass on your left the town clerk's office and the road onto which you turned at the beginning of the trip. Continue STRAIGHT, passing the Greensboro Health Center on the right.

26.7   You have arrived back at The Willey's Store and owe yourself a treat to something inside. The store is a wonderful example of a real country store, well stocked with anything you might wish to buy. The public beach is across the road from the store.

Accommodations
The Highland Lodge, Caspian Lake, Greensboro, VT 05762 (802-533-2647).
An elegant country inn with a lodge and ten cottages. Full dining area and a sandy beach.
The Rodgers Dairy Farm, Glover, VT 05762 (802-525-6677).
An 1840 farmhouse on a working 350-acre dairy farm. Limited to ten guests for the five available rooms, with great views.

Camping
Groton State Forest, Groton, VT 05046.
Picnicking, fishing, hunting, hiking, tent sites, trailer sites, hot showers, nature trail, nature center.

Bicycle Service
Park Pedals, South Walden Road, Cabot, VT (802-563-2252).

Orleans

Distance: 26.1 miles
Difficulty: Strenuous
Riding surface: Primarily gravel, with a small amount of pavement
Towns included: Orleans, Barton, Brownington, Coventry, Derby, Newport
Map: USGS 15' Memphremagog

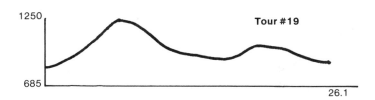

The Indian name for the area that is now the town of Orleans was "Kweekomkwak," which means, "a place to fish for suckers." Located near the confluence of the Barton and Willoughby rivers, Orleans' piscatorial reputation has improved considerably thanks to the fine steelhead trout fishing enjoyed each spring in the Willoughby.

The town's first English name, given upon its settlement in 1821, was Barton's Landing. In 1909, the citizens changed the name to Orleans, supposedly to separate the identity of their village from that of nearby Barton. Something of a rivalry developed between the two villages, and athletic contests of the past sometimes erupted into brawls.

Furniture making has long been a principle industry in Orleans because of the village's proximity to large stands of hardwoods. Many of the country's piano sounding boards were produced in Orleans in the past, and the Ethan Allen factory makes fine hardwood furniture today.

0.0 The departure point for this trip is in the village of Orleans, in front of the Greenwood Store. With the store on your left and the Ethan Allen factory across the street to your right, proceed down Main Street. Bear right across the bridge, pass the Valley House Inn on your left, and take VT 58 out of town.

0.4 Stay RIGHT at this intersection, continuing on VT 58.

0.8 Continue STRAIGHT past Desmarais Equipment Sales.

1.5 Turn LEFT onto a dirt road marked by a sign as Country Club Road;

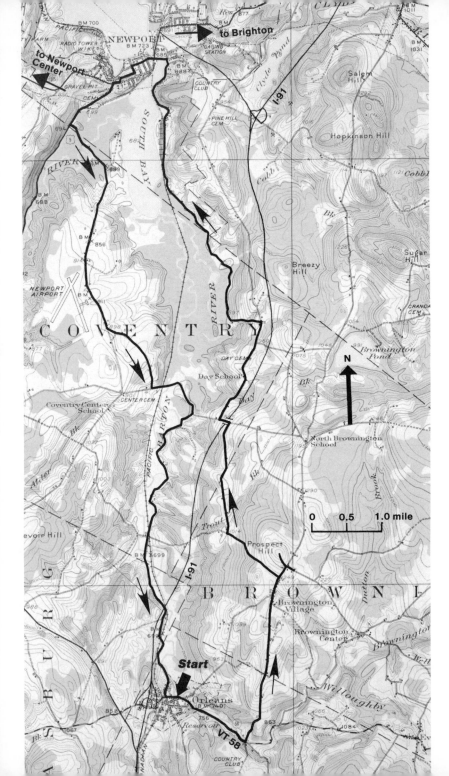

there also is a sign here for Walker's Tree Farm. Begin a climb of nearly a mile, passing on the left almost immediately a newly constructed house with attractive stone siding. The washboard surface of the first half mile of this climb is particularly rough, but the road surface improves after that.

2.5 Pass the Walker Tree Farm.

3.7 At this point, the road becomes paved and climbs into the settlement of Brownington. A sign at the top discusses the famous stone house, Athenian Hall.

In the early years of the nineteenth century, Brownington was on an important stagecoach route between Boston and Canada. The handful of handsome houses and church adjacent to the Old Stone House speak to the prosperity of the past. Brownington, as did many of the original Vermont hill settlements, fell victim to progress as railway lines laid through the valleys replaced the network of stagecoach routes in the mid-1800s.

4.1 Turn RIGHT just past the sign to visit the house, visible to the right just a few hundred feet ahead. (**Note:** Do not detach odometer for this side trip. The trip mileage includes a visit to the Stone House, as well as a visit to the observatory across the road.)

The Reverend Alexander Twilight, shortly after graduating from Middlebury College, was hired as principal of the local academy in 1829. Because an increasing number of his students were coming from quite a distance to be schooled, Reverend Twilight besought the school trustees for a new building in which his scholars could be housed and fed. They refused, and the Reverend set about erecting a new building on his own — with only the help of a single ox and a few willing neighbors, as the story goes. Quarrying the granite on his own land nearby, he proceeded to adapt the system used by the Egyptians in building their pyramids to construct this building. The system made use of an earthen ramp wrapped around the building so he could reach the top. The earth ramp was peeled away once the walls were in place.

With a parlor, dining room, and fireplace-equipped kitchen on the first floor, tiny student rooms on the second, and assembly hall and library on the third, the facility operated for twenty years but closed soon after the Reverend's death in 1857. Although used somewhat as a lodging facility for the next fifty years, the building gradually declined until it was purchased by the Orleans County Historical Society in 1916. It remains in the society's care to this day and contains excellent displays of tools, furniture, and other artifacts of the past.

In addition to the monumental accomplishment that Athenian

The Brownington schoolmaster constructed this building nearly singlehandedly after town fathers denied his request for money for a new school.

Hall represents, Reverend Twilight is believed to have been America's first black college graduate and its first black legislator.

Leaving the Stone House, return to the intersection where you turned. Across the road to the right, on the top of the hill, is the Prospect Hill Observatory. Cross the road and climb the slight grade to the observatory.

A small wooden platform tower owned by the Vermont Historical Society and leased by the Orleans County Historical Society, the observatory offers a superb view of the surrounding countryside. Lake Memphremagog can be seen to the north, stretching into Canada, and the Lake Willoughby region is visible to the south.

Descending back to the main road from the observatory access road, turn RIGHT, passing the Stone House to your left and heading back in the direction from which you came. You'll be taking the first road on your right.

5.0 Turn RIGHT, directly across the road from a red barn, passing a white mobile home with brown trim on the right as you make the turn.

6.0 Follow the road as it bends to the RIGHT, passing on your left first a road and then a log home.

6.5 Pass on the left a trail going into a field.

7.6 Turn LEFT, and cross the I-91 overpass bridge. Prepare to take your first right on the other side of the bridge.

7.7 Turn RIGHT.

8.5 Be alert for loose dogs in this area as you pass a white mobile home behind which is a red barn.

8.7 Pass a cemetery on the right.

9.3 Turn LEFT onto the road directly across from the Hillcrest Dairy Farm and glide downhill for a half mile.

11.1 Pass a sign on your left indicating that you have left the town of Coventry and arrived in Newport City.

11.6 The road now becomes paved. Labeled as Glenn Street at the other end, this road will take you into the city of Newport.

11.9 Pass on the left some Agway petroleum tanks, and note that the southernmost finger of Lake Memphremagog can be seen on the left.

12.4 Pass a railroad yard on the left.

14.0 Bear LEFT, passing Fern Street on the right.

14.1   Turn LEFT onto Mt. Vernon Street. Lake Memphremagog is on your right, and the city of Newport before you.

Newport is situated at the southern extreme of Lake Memphremagog, a name that to the Abenaki Indians meant "beautiful water." It is indeed a beautiful lake, and large as well, stretching thirty miles north into Canada with about a third of it in Vermont, and being four-miles wide in places.

Long an attraction for Indian fishing and hunting parties from Canada, Lake Memphremagog was first seen by white men in 1752. The men, John Stark and Amos Eastman, were Indian prisoners who had been captured in New Hampshire. They were eventually ransomed for a total of $163.

In 1759 during the French and Indian War, John Stark passed through the area again as a lieutenant in Robert Rogers Rangers, a rough-and-tumble provincial military regiment. The Rangers were retreating from a surprise attack on the St. Francis Indians in Canada where, inflamed by the sight of several hundred white scalps hanging about the village, they had killed two hundred men, women, and children. One group of the Rangers was overtaken and killed by pursuing Indians near what is now Newport, and the rest made their way with great hardship to the Connecticut River and eventually to safety downstream.

One hundred years ago, Newport was a booming lumber town and home to a large mill owned by Prouty and Miller, one of the largest lumber companies in the East. Water near the mill's shoreline was often choked with logs that had been floated in for processing. Further out, elegant steamships that were manufactured locally plied the lake to provide transportation for vacationers.

The modern Newport is an active small city providing a variety of services to the more isolated Northeast Kingdom communities. Lake Memphremagog holds nearly every kind of fish to be found in Vermont, and is popular with fishermen as well as with boaters and swimmers. Every July the city of Newport holds the annual Aquafest, a gala celebration focused on the lake and featuring a twenty-six-mile swimming race.

If you wish to stop here for lunch, The Landing on Lake Street is a restaurant that overlooks the lake. Ask for directions in town.

14.3   Turn LEFT at the intersection in front of the Poulin Grain Building and head up Main Street, passing almost immediately on the left the Visual Effects Store and the Stevens Real Estate office.

14.6   Turn LEFT onto School Street at this busy intersection, and begin looking for signs to US 5 South and the airport.

14.8   Turn RIGHT onto Pleasant Street, following the signs to the airport and

US 5 South. Climb the Pleasant Street Hill, and note the big stone church on the left.

The twin-spired granite church belongs to the parish of Saint Mary's and was built in 1909. Romanesque in appearance and with an interior featuring intricate paintings of Biblical scenes by a French painter named Rochon, the church commands one of the best views to be had of Lake Memphremagog and the surrounding area.

15.2 Turn LEFT, still following the airport/US 5 South signs, and continue STRAIGHT, passing a road on the left in about a half mile.

16.0 Turn LEFT onto the road marked by a sign as the way to the airport. Within a couple hundred feet of the turn, you pass on the left the town boundary sign indicating that you are no longer in Newport City, but rather in Coventry.

16.4 Cross over the Barton River on a bridge with cement siding.

17.8 Pass the Armela Farm on the left, and in the next few miles pass several other working and prosperous-looking dairy farms.

With the surrounding fields stretching away on rolling hills, farms in this area of Vermont have a different appearance from the farms that cling to abrupt hillsides in other parts of the state. There are fine views to the left from this stretch.

18.7 Pass the Newport Airport, a small, state-operated facility on the right.

19.3 Turn LEFT off the paved road toward the Neighborhood Farm, distinctive because of its four silos and red barn.

19.5 Pass on your left the Neighborhood Farm.

20.3 With trees close on either side, the road dips sharply before intersecting with another road.

20.4 Turn LEFT at this intersection.

20.6 Cross the railroad tracks, then a bridge over the Barton River.

21.3 Turn RIGHT at this intersection.

21.6 Pass a private road on the left.

23.5 Cross the railroad tracks, and continue STRAIGHT ahead past roads on both the left and the right.

23.7 Cross a steel bridge.

23.8 Cross a cement bridge.

24.6 Pass under the I-91 overpass.

25.0   Pass on the right the Riendeau slaughterhouse and cross the railroad tracks; the road now becomes paved.

25.4   Once again cross the Barton River, and pass on the left the Indian Point Fishing Access.

25.7   Pass through a neighborhood with houses lining both sides of the street.

25.9   This is the intersection near the center of town that you passed earlier. Turn RIGHT, and proceed to the Greenwood Store starting point just ahead.

26.1   You are back at the starting point.

Accommodations

The Valley House Inn, 4 Memorial Square, Orleans, VT 05860 (802-754-6665).
    A big, handsome, wooden hotel that maintains the original charm of the past. Reasonable rates.

Camping

Brighton State Park, Island Pond, VT 05846.
    Picnic tables and fireplaces, swimming, boating, fishing, hiking, tent sites, lean-tos, and hot showers.

Bicycle Service

East Burke Sports, Inc., Box 189, Rt. 118, East Burke, VT (802-626-3215).
Gagnon Sports, 25 Railroad Avenue, Orleans, VT (802-754-6466).
Great Outdoors Trading Company, 73 Main Street, Newport, VT (fifteen miles from starting point) (802-334-2831). Sales, service.
Village Sport Shop, Rural Route 5, Lyndonville, VT (802-626-8448).

Lake Willoughby

Distance: 24.7 miles
Difficulty: Strenuous
Riding surface: Maintained gravel, with a small amount of pavement
Towns included: Charleston, Westmore, Newark, Brighton
Maps: USGS 15' Island Pond, Memphremagog, Lyndonville, Burke

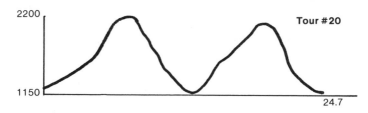

Island Pond gets its name from the circular twenty-two-acre island located in its center. The lake is two-miles long and about a mile and a half wide, encompasses more than six hundred acres, and offers fine fishing for brown trout, rainbow trout, pickerel, and bass. One of the lake's unusual features is that its outlet, the Clyde River, is able under high water conditions to reverse its flow and become an inlet stream. It will then reverse itself again and resume its proper role as the outlet.

This area was settled originally in 1822, a relatively late settlement because of its distance from other settled areas. Before roads were constructed, supplies had to be transported west the sixteen miles from the Connecticut River. During the winter when the snow was too deep for a team of oxen, supplies had to be retrieved on snowshoes and transported on a hand sled.

The railroad track was laid through town in 1853, making Island Pond the first international train depot in the country and connecting the large commercial entities of Montreal and Portland, Maine. At the time, winter traffic on the St. Lawrence River was impossible because of ice, and the train provided a cold-weather connection to the open Atlantic in Portland. The quiet village became an instant boom town, and for the next fifty years the railroad was the town's chief benefactor, providing a steady flow of money to boost the local economy and a regular stream of worldly travelers whose constant presence enriched it culturally. Manufacturing activity was strong as well, with the Gane Shirt Company employing 125 people and producing a thousand shirts a day, as well as the neck bands and cuffs that were popular at the time.

A major expansion was implemented around 1900 that created an additional two hundred jobs, but the best years were past and the village began its decline in 1912. The last train passed through town in 1967, and the population diminished by nearly a thousand soon after.

In recent years, Island Pond has gained statewide recognition because of the presence of the Northeast Kingdom Church, a cult-like group that moved to town in 1978, bought nearly two dozen buildings, and started several businesses including the Common Sense Restaurant. Townspeople became uneasy over rumors about church doctrine, including a belief that children should be disciplined with strict physical punishment. Concern for the children resulted in a startling early morning raid on the commune by ninety Vermont State Police in 1984, a move that resulted in the state assuming custody of 110 church children for their protection. The raid was soon ruled illegal by the courts, and the children were returned to their families.

Today, Island Pond is a popular recreation spot, and the town's brochure reminds visitors that Brighton is the birthplace of Rudy Vallee.

To reach the starting point of the trip, leave Island Pond heading west toward the intersection of VT 105 and VT 114. Park at the gravel turnoff here.

0.0 Start at the gravel turnoff across from the intersection of VT 105 and VT 114. With VT 114 on your left, head west on VT 105.

3.2 Turn LEFT off VT 105.

3.6 Turn LEFT again, passing a barn on the left and a house on the right as you make this turn.

3.9 Cross Mud Brook, and continue to climb.

4.4 Keep to the LEFT.

4.7 Pass on your left an interesting residence that appears to be two houses built close together, each with a different roof style, that were joined.

4.8 Bear RIGHT, passing a private road on the left.

4.9 Turn RIGHT at the intersection.

5.3 To your left are excellent views of Northeast Kingdom terrain stretching to the northeast.

5.7 Goodwin Mountain is to the left, at more than 2,900 feet; the road dips deeply here.

7.1 This is the height of land, and the edge of the world seems to be just ahead as the land drops away steeply on the other side.

This is one of the finest views in Vermont, with spectacular Lake

Willoughby in the foreground and majestic mountain ranges beyond. A fast descent begins here.

8.1 Pavement begins, and the downward drop continues.

9.5 Turn LEFT onto VT 5A at this intersection, with the Westmore Community Hall and Community Church on your right, and the old school (1857) on the left.

Westmore was originally settled in the early 1800s but was abandoned in 1812 as settlers sought greater protection at the outbreak of the War of 1812 with Britain. It was resettled in 1830, and until the present the town's identity has been woven inextricably with that of the majestic Lake Willoughby.

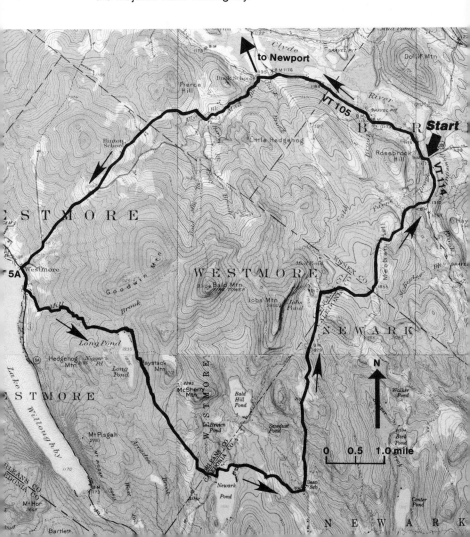

Five-miles long, up to a mile and a half wide, and over three-hundred-feet deep, Lake Willoughby cuts distinctively between the sheer cliff faces of Mount Hor and Mount Pisgah. Unusual arctic plants live on the latter. This deep, cold lake is a favorite of Vermont fishermen and yields huge rainbow and lake trout and landlocked salmon. The state recordholding lake trout was caught here in 1981, a fish nearly four-feet long and weighing thirty-four pounds.

As with many of Vermont's larger lakes, an active resort community has flourished at Lake Willoughby for the last one hundred years, first with hotels and more recently with private camps.

9.9   Turn LEFT at the Millbrook Gift Store.

10.2 After an initial steep climb, the ascent becomes more "stepped" with plateaus.

10.5 Continue STRAIGHT past a private drive on the left.

11.7 Continue STRAIGHT past a road on the right, and shortly after begin a downhill run.

12.0 Long Pond is on the right, complete with its small island.
Covering more than one hundred acres, this pond holds both brook and lake trout. Although overshadowed by the sheer magnificence of Lake Willoughby, the three smaller ponds you will view along here are each very attractive in their own right.

12.1 Continue STRAIGHT past a snowmobile trail on the left and circle above the shore of the pond.

12.8 Pass a private drive on your right.

13.7 Pass another private drive on your right.

13.8 Continue STRAIGHT past a trail on the left.

15.0 Turn LEFT onto Town Highway 13 (marked here by a sign), passing a snowmobile trail continuing to the right.

15.3 Continue STRAIGHT past a trail on the left.

15.4 Turn LEFT at Newark Pond.
This pond holds brook trout in its 163 acres.

15.8 Pass the Newark Pond Fishing Access on the right. Follow the road as it bends to the right, passing Town Highway 10 on the left, and proceed straight on Town Highway 11. There is a cluster of camps on either side of the road at this point.

17.2 Turn LEFT onto the pavement, and make a short quarter-mile climb past the Bald Hill Fish Hatchery on the left. The road reverts back to gravel at the top of this rise.

The Bald Hill Fish Hatchery provides a good place to take a break. This hatchery specializes in raising landlocked salmon and steelhead rainbow trout.

20.2 Pass a sign on your left announcing that you have left the town of Newark and are now in Westmore.

20.3 Job's Pond access road is on the left.

This handsome little pond holding brook trout is worth a quick visit. Fifty years ago, there was a family summer camp at the far end of the pond that offered swimming, tennis, boating, fishing, and child care to its limit of thirty-five guests.

20.7 Continue STRAIGHT past a trail on the left.

21.0 Pass a sign on the right proclaiming that you have departed Westmore and are now back in the town of Newark.

The town boundaries intersect in an angular fashion in this vicinity, making it possible to leave one town and then enter it again in a short distance.

21.6 Continue STRAIGHT past a road on the right.

21.8 Bear to the LEFT, passing a trail on the right.

23.0 The road is paved here, and a rapid descent is ahead.

23.8 Turn LEFT onto VT 114.

24.7 Once again you have reached the intersection of VT 105 and VT 114 from which you began this trip.

Accommodations

The Lakefront Motel, 4 Cross Street, Island Pond, VT 05846 (802–723–6507).

A new two-story motel built on the shore of Island Pond and in the center of the village. Adjacent to tennis courts, beach, and children's playground. Some units available with built-in kitchenettes.

Camping

Brighton State Park, Island Pond, VT 05846.

Picnic tables and fireplaces, swimming, boating, fishing, hiking, tent sites, lean-tos, and hot showers.

Bicycle Service

Great Outdoors Trading Company, 73 Main Street, Newport, VT (802–334–2831). Sales, service.

Ferdinand

Distance: 15.6 miles round trip
Difficulty: Easy/Moderate
Riding surface: Maintained gravel
Towns included: Ferdinand, Lewis
Map: USGS 15' Island Pond

This out-and-back trip penetrates the remote northern bog country of the Northeast Kingdom using a logging road. The grade rises very gradually on the first half of the trip, and there are no steep ascents, although the grade of the first mile or so is a little steeper than the rest of the trip. The road is wide enough at the beginning to accommodate two large trailer trucks packed with logs but, by the time you reach the turn-around, will have deteriorated considerably.

Logging trucks have the right of way on this road, and they won't be expecting bicyclists. Use caution and keep alert. When you hear a truck approaching in the distance, get off the road and let it pass.

Most of the land here is owned by a paper company, but the logging is carried out by independent contractors. Equipped with chain saws and huge tractor-like machines called log skidders, the loggers are a hearty breed who carry on the tradition of a difficult and dangerous trade. You may come across a "landing" where logs are processed and stacked, and if so you will have the opportunity to see them at work. At any landing you encounter, stop well away from the work area and size up what's going on. Additional heavy equipment may be at work, and the road may be muddy, so proceed through only during a lull in the work or when the equipment operators have noticed you and have indicated that it is safe to pass.

The wood being cut here is called pulp wood and will be used by the paper company to make paper products. Traditionally, twenty- to thirty-foot logs are cut into four-foot sections for transportation to the mill. In the past, the logger used his chain saw to cut each log individually into the four-foot pieces, but a recent innovation processes the logs mechanically. An operator sits in an enclosed pivoting cab mounted on a trailer, similar in appearance to an excavator cab. By maneuvering a jointed boom with large log hooks mounted at the end, the operator picks up full-length logs a half dozen at a time and places them on the back end of the trailer below the cab. When he has a dozen or more logs in a pile on the trailer, he activates a huge five-foot saw blade mounted perpendicular to the logs. The saw cuts the dozen logs into twelve four-foot sections like a knife through butter, and does it in the same amount of time it would have taken the logger with his chain saw to cut a single piece. You may see one of these machines in operation at a landing.

This is prime big game country, and you will very likely see the tracks of moose and deer along the road. If you are lucky, you may even see a live one. The moose population of Vermont has increased considerably in recent years, and sightings are fairly common. Although smaller than moose in Alaska and other big wilderness areas, Vermont adult males may weigh a half ton or more, sporting heavy, flattened antlers that are up to four feet from tip to tip.

With excellent hearing and a keen sense of smell to compensate for its poor eyesight, a moose will sense your presence from quite a distance. Frequently they like to hang out in the swamps, where rolling in mud and water can provide relief from biting insects, and to make daily feeding forays onto the surrounding ridges to feast on the young trees growing there. They also enjoy a variety of aquatic plants and can sometimes be seen feeding along the shores of ponds or streams.

Even though they are considered docile most of the time, bulls are known to be aggressive during the fall mating season, and there have been several reports in recent years of unsuspecting Vermont outdoorsmen forced to beat a hasty retreat to a nearby tree or vehicle when a bull has mistaken them for a romantic competitor.

To reach the starting point of this trip, take VT 105 East from Island Pond about 7 miles or so. Just past a camp situated close to the highway and clearly labeled "Hardwick Camp, Wenlock Station," and on the opposite side of the road, is a large gravel pulloff into which enters a logging road coming out of the forest. Just beyond this pulloff is where the railroad tracks cross the highway, so if you find yourself crossing tracks, you've gone too far.

The directions for this trip are quite simple, for there are no other roads in the area.

0.0 Begin this trip on the gravel turnoff and enter the forest on the logging road.

The Nulhegan River's North Branch leaves the forest to join the Nulhegan near this starting point. The proximity of that junction calls to mind a story that happened near this spot that exemplifies the pioneer spirit of frontier settlers everywhere:

Before roads were built in this area, winter travel was done on snowshoes. One late winter day, a young man named Timothy Hinman set out from the Connecticut River some sixteen miles

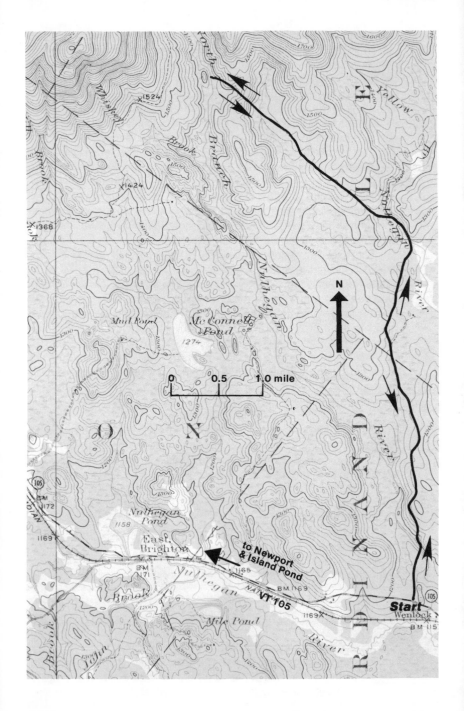

away. The day was warm, and the melting snow clung to his moccasins and made the traveling slow. As the sun began to sink low in the afternoon sky, Mr. Hinman found that his feet were soaking wet, his destination was still a considerable distance, and the temperature was dropping dangerously. Before long, his moccasins were freezing solid, and he knew that if he did not take immediate action his feet were in danger of freezing as well. Hinman had reached the Nulhegan, and, in desperation to save his feet, he pried off his frozen moccasins and placed his feet in the river where the flowing water was above freezing. There he spent the night. In the morning, he bandaged his feet with cloth, strapped on his snowshoes, and completed his trip, apparently none the worse for the experience.

0.2 Follow the road as it bends sharply past a private drive on the right.

4.3 Turn LEFT at the intersection.

7.0 The road begins to deteriorate at this point, becoming more narrow and rough and with grass growing from the middle. Continue ahead.

7.8 This is the end point, marked by a wide snowmobile bridge crossing the North Branch of the Nulhegan River to your left. Retrace your route to return to the starting point.

This is a pleasant spot to have a picnic or to try your luck angling for the native brook trout in the cold, clear stream.

If you were to continue straight on the trail, you would come across a camp not far ahead on land that is leased by the paper company to a private individual. Past the camp, the trail disappears and the terrain becomes very muddy and impassable. If you cross the bridge and continue on that trail, you will intersect with another major logging road in about a half mile.

However, no scouting has been done beyond this point, and it is important to stress that this is not the place for casual exploration. It is a huge and inhospitable wilderness, and you should stick to the trail described here.

15.6 You have now reached the starting point.

Accommodations

The Lakefront Motel, 4 Cross Street, Island Pond, VT 05846 (802–723–6507).

A new two-story motel built on the shore of Island Pond and in the center of the village. Adjacent to tennis courts, beach, and children's playground. Some units available with built-in kitchenettes.

Camping

Brighton State Park, Island Pond, VT 05846.

Picnic tables and fireplaces, swimming, boating, fishing, hiking, tent sites, lean-tos, and hot showers.

Bicycle Service

East Burke Sports, Inc., Box 189, Rt. 118, East Burke, VT (802–626–3215).

Gagnon Sports, 25 Railroad Avenue, Orleans, VT (802–754–6466).

Great Outdoors Trading Company, 73 Main Street, Newport, VT (802–334–2831). Sales, service.

Village Bike Shop, Newport Road, Derby, VT (802–766–8009).

Village Sport Shop, Rural Route 5, Lyndonville, VT (802–626–8448).

Northwest Vermont

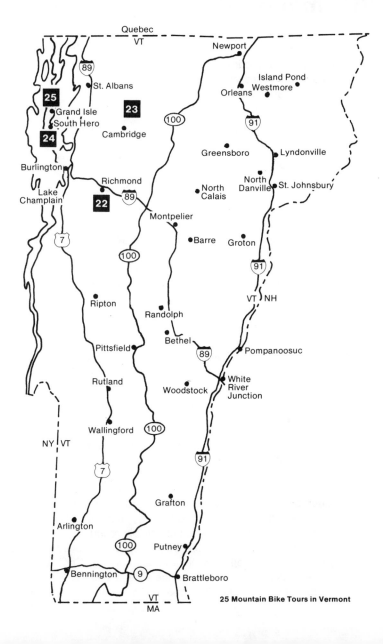

Quebec
VT

Newport

89

St. Albans

Island Pond
Westmore

Orleans

25

Grand Isle
South Hero

23

100

91

Cambridge

Greensboro

Lyndonville

24

Burlington

Richmond

89

North
Calais

North
Danville

St. Johnsbury

Lake
Champlain

22

Montpelier

7

Barre

Groton

100

91

Ripton

VT NH

Randolph

Bethel

Pittsfield

89

Pompanoosuc

Rutland

Woodstock

White
River
Junction

Wallingford

100

NY VT

7

91

Grafton

Arlington

100

Putney

Bennington

9

Brattleboro

VT
MA

25 Mountain Bike Tours in Vermont

Richmond

Distance: 11.4 miles
Difficulty: Moderate
Riding surface: Pavement and gravel roads
Towns included: Richmond
Maps: USGS 15' Burlington, Camel's Hump

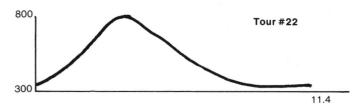

Tour #22

This trip climbs into the hills south of Richmond Village, passing by Owl's Head Mountain and providing a breathtaking view of Camel's Hump. The latter portion of the trip escorts the Huntington River on its four-mile dash to the Winooski, then follows the latter west over rolling river bottomland back to the starting point.

Start in the village of Richmond at the recreation field next to the Winooski River. You'll find a band shell, playground equipment, and parking space at the field. There is a good variety of businesses in town, but one in particular that draws faithful customers from afar is the Daily Bread Cafe and Bakery, where you can try maple bread among other delights.

0.0 Leave the recreation area, turn RIGHT, and cross the bridge over the Winooski River.

0.2 Keep to the RIGHT, passing on your left the village green and the Old Round Church, completed in 1813. Just past the green, bear right sharply following the sign for Huntington.

Although the Old Round Church took only two years to build, it took sixteen previous years for townspeople to agree on the actual site. The issue was settled only after two local businessmen donated land.

The Old Round Church is not actually round but sixteen-sided. It is popularly believed that the construction style of the building was dictated by the cooperative effort of the seventeen men who erected it. One man was held responsible for each of the sixteen sides, and the seventeenth was responsible for the octagonal belfry. Others believe that the head

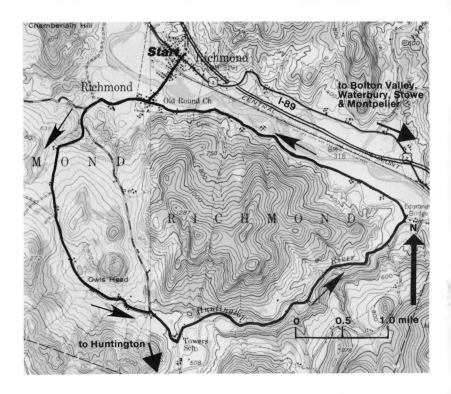

carpenter, who was also the town's blacksmith and whose work on the church was done without pay, had been inspired by a similar sixteen-sided building near the home of his youth in New Hampshire. Still others say that a sixteen-sided building leaves no corners where your enemies or the devil can hide.

The total cost of $2,300 (with $36 going for the eighteen thousand shingles) was offset by selling pews. Use of the church for services was then apportioned in equal amounts to the faiths contributing the most, which were the Congregationalists with twenty-nine pews committed and the Universalists with twenty-one. At the other end of the scale were the Christians and Baptists with five pews each, and one pew for the single Methodist. There are no reports on how the lone Methodist soul used his time allotment. The Old Round Church is believed to be the first in the country to use this cooperative community approach in its construction.

Henry Ford at one time expressed interest in buying this church for his Dearborn, Michigan, museum, but negotiations were never successfully completed.

1.0 Keep to the LEFT, still following the sign to Huntington, and begin climbing a steep hill; the total climb is about a mile. The route to this point remains paved.

A unique octagonal silo shows that farm architecture can take many interesting shapes.

1.2 Turn RIGHT onto a paved road, and continue to climb up a hill and through a development of recent-vintage houses.

1.7 The road turns to dirt at this point.

2.1 Continue STRAIGHT past a road on your right. By now, the road levels off and begins to descend.

3.3 Pass on your right the Owl's Head Berry Farm, with extensive plantings of blueberries and raspberries visible on the lower slopes of the hillside in the distance.

4.0 Turn RIGHT onto pavement.

4.5 Turn LEFT onto dirt road, and notice the Huntington River on your right. This is an attractive stream that offers good trout fishing, with some bass further down near the mouth of the river.

6.0 Signs begin to appear along the roadside that prohibit the parking of vehicles, and just ahead you reach the Huntington Gorge.

Huntington Gorge is a beautiful natural phenomenon featuring a powerful waterfall and many potholes. The site is ideal for pothole formation, which requires a swift current and a sudden drop in stream elevation over an uneven bedrock surface. This results in the formation of eddies, in which the swirling motion of the water and captive pebbles act as cutting tools to drill the smooth, cylindrical shapes.

Just below the falls on the bank near the road you can still see the foundation remnants of the old spoke factory that occupied the site in the 1880s and 1890s. The business included a grist and cider mill and also made clothespins and wooden handles for files and ice picks. For some reason, the mill turned to making underwear in the 1890s, but before then production of the original commodities peaked at 1.4 million spokes and 400 barrels of cider annually.

Some of those barrels might have been for the Bunker brothers, Sam and Dodipher, who are part of a local legend equivalent to that about Paul Bunyon. Each of these brothers was well over six-feet tall, weighed over three hundred pounds, and had to pass through doorways turned sideways. One is said to have killed with a single blow from his ax a bear that tried to steal his lunch, and both could lift a keg of cider single-handedly — even lift and drink from a cider keg weighing more than six hundred pounds.

There is a darker side to the Huntington Gorge that makes the place as insidious as it is romantic. Over the years, approximately thirty persons have drowned while swimming here. The same strong currents and eddies that effectively make potholes pull unsuspecting swimmers underwater and trap them under rock ledges in the swirling crosscurrents. It is a very dangerous place to swim.

6.3   Pass "Paramount Farms, Morgans of Distinction."

7.9   Turn LEFT onto a paved road.

As you travel along this road back to the starting point, the Winooski River will be on your right, and across the valley beyond the river is I-89 and the Bolton Mountain Range.

11.1   Turn RIGHT and pass the village green and the round church that you passed at the beginning of the trip. A granite marker commemorating the Cochran family marks the location of this turn.

This Vermont family of skiers are famous for their gold medal Olympic skiing, and they operate a small, family-oriented ski area nearby.

11.4   The trip is complete as you reach the starting point.

Accommodations

Camel's Hump Nordic Ski Center, R.D.1, Box 99, Huntington, VT 05462 (802–434–2704).

Rustic ambiance, spectacular views, modest facilities, friendly spot for family fun.

The Black Bear Inn, Mountain Road, Bolton Valley, VT 05477 (802–434–2126/2920).

Comfortable mountaintop inn with panoramic mountain views, pool, hiking, tennis, indoor sports center.

Camping

Little River State Park, Waterbury, VT 05676.

Picnic tables and fireplaces, swimming, fishing, boat rentals, tent sites, lean-tos, trailer sites, and hot showers.

Bicycle Service

Earle's Schwinn Cyclery, 2500 Williston Road, S. Burlington, VT (802–864–9197); 135 Main Street, Burlington, VT (802–862–4203). Sales and service.

Endurance Sports, 421 Governor Chittenden Road, Williston, VT (802–879–6001).

Essex Junction Bicycles, 50 Pearl Street, Essex Jct., VT (802–878–1275).

Jericho Sports, 7 LaFayette Drive, RR 1 Box 14, Jericho, VT (802–899–3549).

Mountain Bike Shop, Green Mountain Inn, P.O. Box 478, Stowe, VT (802–253–7919).

Mountain Sports, 1056 Mountain Road, Stowe, VT (802–253–4896). Sales and service.

North Star Cyclery, 100 Main Street, Burlington, VT (802–863–3832).

The Ski Rack Bike Shop, 81 Main Street, Burlington, VT (802–658–3313). Sales and service.

Victory Sports, 76 Heineberg Drive, Colchester, VT (802–862–0963).

Winooski Bicycle Shop, 12 W. Canal Street, P.O. Box 152, Winooski, VT (802–655–3233).

Cambridge

Distance: 24.7 miles
Difficulty: Strenuous
Riding surface: Mostly gravel, some pavement
Towns included: Cambridge, Fletcher, Fairfield, Bakersfield,
Maps: USGS 15' Mount Mansfield, Enosburg Falls

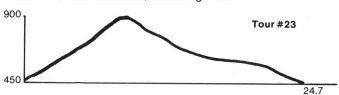

This is an enjoyable trip that winds through the hills north of the Lamoille River. It offers great local scenery as well as outstanding views of the omnipresent Mount Mansfield, Vermont's highest mountain at 4,393 feet, to the south.

The day's journey begins in the village of Cambridge, an attractive and stable community situated on a low, flat piece of land on the banks of the Lamoille River. The main thoroughfare of Cambridge is unusually wide, a result of an early example of prudent city planning. In laying out the main street, the town fathers opted for a space big enough for the local military unit to drill without interfering with traffic.

The first blow of a settler's ax against a tree in Cambridge came in 1783, when a lone man came in the spring, cleared two acres of land along the river, and planted corn. In early fall, the river, swelled by the annual heavy fall rains, poured over its banks and washed away most of the corn that had ripened. Undaunted, the man returned the following spring with his wife and two children where they took up residence in a log house that had no windows and only a quilt for a door throughout the entire first winter.

0.0 Begin in front of the Cambridge Post Office at the Cambridge Market Place, with the post office on your right. Proceed onto the main road (VT 15), passing the handsome brick Cambridge Inn on your right. Follow the road as it bends around the corner to your left, passing the Mount Mansfield American Legion building on your right. Cross the bridge over the Lamoille River.

Although it is a pleasant-sounding word that is full of promise, Lamoille (pronounced La Moyle) doesn't have any meaning in

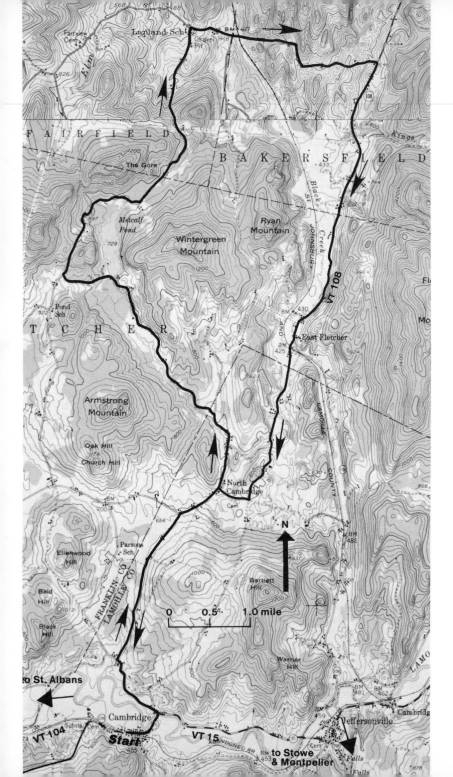

French. Rather, it is an adaptation of the French word La Mouette, meaning gull. The proliferation of those birds at the river's mouth prompted Samuel Champlain, who discovered the river while exploring Lake Champlain in 1609, to call it La Mouette. Over the years, La Mouette inexplicably became Lamoille.

The river offers fine canoeing in summer as well as spring, a time when many Vermont rivers often are too low for navigation. It supports a rich variety of fish, including trout, pike, and bass.

0.4 Turn LEFT.

0.5 Continue STRAIGHT past a road going to the right.

1.3 Turn RIGHT onto Town Highway 7.

1.8 Pass the Cambridge Herbary on your left.
The Cambridge Herbary grows and sells eighty-eight different kinds of herbs. You can also buy dried wreaths, potpourri, perfumes, teas, vinegars, and various books relating to the subject. Since you will pass the herbary on the return trip, you may wish to postpone a stop and subsequent purchases until then.

2.3 Pass a sign for Cambridge Stained Glass and Woodworking on the right.

3.3 Keep to the RIGHT past a road going to the left.

3.5 Keep to the LEFT past a road going to the right.

3.9 Keep to the LEFT past a road going to the right.

4.4 Continue STRAIGHT past a road on the right.

4.8 Turn LEFT.
Just ahead, you'll pass out of the town of Cambridge and into the town of Fletcher, although the boundary is not marked by any sign.

5.6 Pass a private road on the right and a large marshy area on the left that continues for nearly a mile.

5.8 Continue STRAIGHT past roads on both the left and right.
This peaceful country road is in the vicinity of a brutal murder that occurred in September of 1855. Jefferson Fulton and Abial Chase lived near here on adjacent farms and for years had disputed the location of the boundary lines. On the fateful morning of the murder, Chase brought the situation to a head when he fortified himself with rum and a sharp butcher knife and set out for the Fulton farm. He came upon Jefferson Fulton and his ten-year-old son making fence poles near the house and attacked the elder, plunging the butcher knife into his chest. The victim reeled backward and spun around to flee, but Chase thrust the knife into his back to kill him. The assailant

then turned on the boy, who managed to escape and report the crime to neighbors. A watch was put on all roads in the area and on the railway station, and a search party was organized that scoured the surrounding hills for the killer. Chase was found by a search party two days later cowering in a nearby swamp. When he found himself surrounded and without chance for escape, he proceeded to commit suicide by slashing his own throat with an old, dull jackknife. Where he had hidden for two days remains a mystery, but some believed he hid in a nearby cave (see below).

Today, many Vermont towns retain the elected public office of Fence Viewer for the purpose of settling property line disputes.

7.1 Metcalf Pond is on the right, with an island on the distant end. Continue on as the road veers away from the pond and begins a climb of a half mile.

7.8 Turn RIGHT at this intersection.

9.2 Here the road passes close by the northernmost end of Metcalf Pond, showing the back side of the island you viewed previously as well as the southern view of the pond.

There is a cave near here where the infamous Abial Chase is thought to have hidden from the search party, and where other fugitives hid out in the past as well. Although I have not visited the cave, it might make an interesting side trip. The cave is supposed to be north of Metcalf Pond in the side of a hill, facing south and with the entrance near the base of the hill. In other words, it should be to your left as you bicycle through this area. The passage into the cave is reported to be narrow but high, and about one hundred-feet long. The chamber is at a lower level, and supposedly there are openings that lead to additional chambers on the same level and lower down.

10.6 Pass a large junkyard on the right. There are dogs at the junkyard that you may want to be alert for, but since they are a distance from the road you should be able to pass quickly and uneventfully.

11.3 The land opens up into farm meadows on both sides of the road.

11.9 Turn RIGHT at this intersection. Climb a brief rise and pass a gravel pit on the right.

12.5 Keep to the LEFT at this intersection, and cross first Black Creek and then railway tracks. Begin a climb.

13.5 Here the land is cleared for a pasture on the right, and there is a spectacular view of the northern face of 4,393-foot Mount Mansfield in the distance. This is Vermont's tallest mountain.

14.6 Turn RIGHT onto paved VT 108.

The Vermont farmers who have given the state its character are a hardworking and resourceful lot whose numbers are fast dwindling.

16.2   Pass the Misty Morning Sheep Farm on your right.

18.2   Turn RIGHT onto a dirt road, crossing railroad tracks and Black Creek.

18.9   Pass on your left the Chase Gun Shop.

19.6   Turn LEFT at this fork in the road, drop down, and cross Black Creek once again.

20.4   Turn RIGHT, passing just ahead a cemetery on the left.

Although history has not preserved exactly where in town the loss might have occurred, the famous Buffalo Bill Cody once lost a valuable diamond ring somewhere in Cambridge. Cody had become friends with Cambridge leading citizen and military officer Daniel Gates during the Civil War. Gates invited Cody up to Vermont for some deer and partridge hunting once the war ended. Cody accepted the invitation after the war, and on one of their outings lost the ring. Gates reportedly hired eight men for three weeks to hunt for the ring, but it was never found.

20.8   Turn LEFT at this intersection onto the road you traveled previously.

21.4   Keep to the LEFT.

21.9   Pass a road on the left.

23.4   Turn LEFT once again onto paved road.

24.3   Turn RIGHT at the traffic light, cross back over the Lamoille River, and continue STRAIGHT ahead into Cambridge Village.

24.7   You have arrived back at the Cambridge Post Office.

Accommodations

The Jefferson House, P.O. Box 288, Main Street, Jeffersonville, VT 05464 (802–644–2030).

This is a lovely Victorian home in the heart of a friendly Vermont village. Three comfortable rooms and a full breakfast, convenient to hiking, canoeing, swimming, fishing.

Windridge Inn, Main Street, Jeffersonville, VT 05464 (802–644–8281).

Eighteenth-century character with exposed hewed timbers and antique furnishings. Private tub-shower, tennis courts.

Red Fox Alpine Lodge, Old Mountain Road and VT 108, Jeffersonville, VT 05464 (802–644–8888).

Once an old red church but now a ski lodge, has bunk arrangements to accommodate 114, with some modern bunk rooms for six to twelve people. Swimming pool, lounge, spa, rec room, home-cooked meals

Camping

Smuggler's Notch State Park, Stowe, VT 05672.

Picnic tables and fireplaces, fishing, tent sites, lean-tos, trailer sites, and hot showers.

Bicycle Service

Action Outfitters, R. 1, 931-D, Stowe, VT (802–253–7975).

Kevin Smith's Sport Connection, 38 S. Main, St. Albans, VT (802–868–2511). Sales and service.

Mountain Bike Shop, Green Mountain Inn, P.O. Box 478, Stowe, VT (802–253–7919).

Mountain Sports, Mountain Road, Stowe, VT (802–253–4896). Sales and service.

South Hero

Distance: 12.2 miles
Difficulty: Easy
Riding surface: Well-packed gravel and pavement
Towns included: South Hero
Map: USGS 15' Plattsburg (NY)

This is a relaxing trip, first along the western shore of this attactive island, then winding inland by some famous North Country apple orchards.

South Hero — and the town of North Hero to the north — take their names from Vermont's legendary Allen brothers, General Ethan and Colonel Ira Allen, fiery, colorful leaders of the early settlement years and heroes in the Revolutionary War. But it was their cousin Ebenezer Allen who was the first settler in the town, a pioneer who paddled his raft to shore on the southern tip of the island at what is now appropriately called Allen's Point.

It was from this town that Ethan Allen set out on his last journey on a cold winter morning in February of 1789, destined to die a very ordinary death before the day was done. Ethan had driven his team of horses and wagon over the ice from Burlington the afternoon before on an outing to buy hay and had spent the evening enjoying his host's conversation, food, and drink. On returning home in the morning, he was taken suddenly ill, perhaps from a stroke. He lived only a few more hours and died at the age of fifty-six.

Start from the Apple Farm Market on US 2 in South Hero.

0.0 Turn LEFT onto US 2 as you leave the parking lot and begin traveling north, passing South Street on the left and Hill Road on the right.

2.0 Turn LEFT onto VT 314 North at this busy intersection.

2.8 Turn LEFT onto Eagle Camp Road.

3.3 Turn LEFT onto West Shore Road.

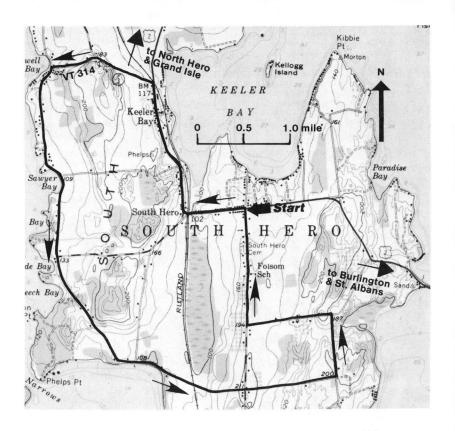

Lake Champlain had been visited by Indians on hunting and fishing expeditions for hundreds of years, but the first white man to lay eyes on it was Samuel Champlain, for whom the lake was named. Arriving in twenty-four canoes in July of 1609 with two countrymen, a party of sixty Algonquin Indians, and all their supplies, Champlain spent three weeks exploring the lake and documenting his observations. Near the end of the month, he was involved in an altercation with hostile Iroquois Indians and killed several of them with his gun — the first firearm the Indians had seen. It was a battle that would have ramifications in the New World for the next 150 years, for the Iroquois thereafter became the allies of the English and the bitter enemies of the French.

4.6 Keep to the RIGHT past a road on the left.

5.5 Continue STRAIGHT past Station Road on your left.

6.8 Pass the Crescent Bay Farm.
  If you're lucky as you gaze out over the water, perhaps you'll catch a glimpse of the Lake Champlain "monster," a phenomenon over

Peaceful roads and apple orchards overlook Lake Champlain in much of South Hero.

which controversy has stirred for years. Sightings of the supposed creature are rare but have occurred regularly for more than three hundred years.

The first white man to view "Champ," as the creature has been nicknamed, was Samuel Champlain during his exploratory expedition to the lake. He reported it to be about five feet long, with heavy scales, a head shaped like that of a horse, and prominent teeth. Indian legends of Champ were similar, but included a report of watching the creature lie quietly next to the shore until birds lit on its snout. It then quickly grabbed them in its jaws.

More recent sightings have reported Champ to be from thirty to fifty feet long, light brown in color, with a body that emerges from the water with two or three humps, a head like a horse, and a neck five feet long and about a foot thick. It is said to travel about fifteen miles an hour, enough to create a small wake.

Some of those who believe such a creature still exists in the dark depths of the lake believe it is the same seen by Champlain, only grown to a larger size. Others feel there may be more than one and that they have reproduced. That Champ is a relative of the Loch Ness monster is popularly believed as well, since both lakes share several characteristics including age, temperature, and depth. One reason given to explain why more sightings have not been reported is that this is a shy, deep dwelling creature that is mostly nocturnal.

7.0 Continue STRAIGHT past Lakeview Road on your left. Providence Island is visible to the right.

Lake Champlain offers some of the finest freshwater fishing in the East. Many of Vermont's record fish have been caught here, including a six-pound bass, a twelve-pound salmon, and a thirty-two-pound catfish. The Lake Champlain Fishing Derby has become an annual event in June, when hundreds of fishermen try their skill at landing the biggest fish and winning the $50,000 grand prize.

8.3 Cross South Street and enter Whipple Road.

9.4 Turn LEFT onto East Shore Road, and pass by the Contentment Farm where horses are raised.

10.0 Turn LEFT onto a paved road.

11.0 Turn RIGHT.

11.2 Pass first the Allenholm Apple Orchard, and then Hackett's Orchard.

This is prime apple growing country, and riding through here during the apple blossom season in early summer is a special treat. Approximately two hundred acres are under cultivation as apple orchards in Grand Isle County, with nearly 100,000 bushels of apples produced annually. About sixty percent of this quantity is MacIntosh apples, with Red Delicious and Cortlands making up much of the rest. These apples can be purchased at the orchard, but most are shipped to other parts of the state and to a broader national market. For years, Vermont MacIntosh apples have been shipped to Europe as well, where they are held in high regard. Plums and cherries are also grown locally, but only in small numbers.

12.2   This is the intersection of US 2, with the Apple Farm Market on the right from which you began the trip.

Accommodations
Sandbar Motor Inn, US 2, South Hero, VT 05486 (802–372–6911).
> Forty lakeside units equipped with phone, TV, heat. Fishing, hiking, windsurfing, and marina. Breakfast and dinner available in casual dining room.

Shore Acres Inn, US 2, North Hero, VT 05474 (802–372–5853).
> Fifty acres of rolling, peaceful, groomed grounds and a half mile of private lake shore. Twenty-three rooms overlooking the lake and distant Green Mountains. Fine country dining in adjacent lakeside restaurant.

Camping
Grand Isle State Park, Grand Isle, VT 05458.
> Picnic tables and fireplaces, swimming, fishing, boating, boat rentals, tent sites, lean-tos, trailer sites, hot showers, rec building.

Bicycle Service
Climb High, Inc., 1861 Shelburne Road, Shelburne, VT (802–985–5056).

Earle's Schwinn Cyclery, 2500 Williston Road, S. Burlington, VT (802–864–9197); 135 Main Street, Burlington, VT (802–862–4203). Sales and service.

Endurance Sports, 421 Governor Chittenden Road, Williston, VT (802–879–6001).

Essex Junction Bicycles, 50 Pearl Street, Essex Jct., VT (802–878–1275).

Island Cyclery, RR 1 Box 557, South Hero, VT (802–372–6619).

Jericho Sports, 7 LaFayette Drive, RR 1 Box 14, Jericho, VT (802–899–3549).

Kevin Smith's Sport Connection, 38 S. Main, St. Albans, VT (802–868–2511). Sales and service.

North Star Cyclery, 100 Main Street, Burlington, VT (802–863–3832).

The Ski Rack Bike Shop, 81 Main Street, Burlington, VT (802–658–3313). Sales and service.

Victory Sports, 76 Heineberg Drive, Colchester, VT (802–862–0963).

Winooski Bicycle Shop, 12 W. Canal Street, P.O. Box 152, Winooski, VT (802–655–3233).

25

Grand Isle

Distance: 18.8 miles
Difficulty: Moderate
Riding surface: Well-packed gravel and pavement
Towns included: Grand Isle
Maps: USGS 15' Rouses Point, Plattsburg (NY)

This route skirts the edges of beautiful Grand Isle, one of four major islands on the north end of Lake Champlain. Beginning on the east side and crossing over to the west, the trip provides unsurpassed views of the lake, the Green Mountains, and the Adirondacks and ambles by several attractive working dairy farms and beautiful residences. Much of the terrain is flat, and the few hills are gradual.

The village of Grand Isle was originally a part of the town of South Hero, but it received its own name and status in 1810, about twenty-seven years after its first settlers. The original settler on this northern part of the island was Alexander Gordon, who built his cabin on the western shore near the current ferry depot at Gordon Landing, which bears his name.

The initial years of settlement in Grand Isle saw development re-stricted to the shoreline. Water from the lake was immediately available for homestead needs, and, equally important, the lake provided a means for transportation and communication. The early watercraft were dugout canoes made Indian-fashion by alternately burning and chiseling out the center of large logs. The first sailing vessel to serve as a ferry to the mainland was put into service in 1800. It was captured by the British during the War of 1812 and partially burned, but it later was refitted and returned to service. By 1828, the community was using a steam-powered ferry. Although the first ferry service to the mainland was not established for seventeen years after the first settler, Grand Isle was equipped with two taverns after only eight years, by 1791.

Most community histories in Vermont reveal that the construction of mills was among the first essential acts of settlement. Sawmills were

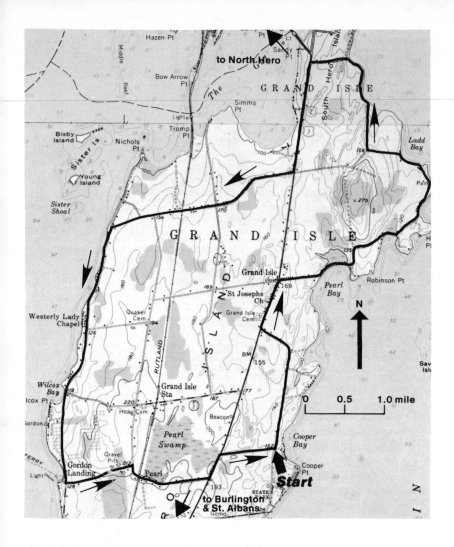

Hazen Pt

to North Hero

GRAND ISLE

Bow Arrow Pt

The

Simms Pt

Lighte

Tromp Pt

Bixby Island

Nichols Pt

Sister Is

Young Island

Sister Shoal

GRAND ISLE

Grand Isle

St Josephs Ch

Westerly Lady Chapel

Quaker Cem

Grand Isle Cem

BM 155

Wilcox Bay

Icox Pt

Grand Isle Sta

Hoag Cem

Gordon

Pearl Swamp

Gravel Pits

Gordon Landing

Light

Pearl

to Burlington & St. Albans

South Hero

Ladd Bay

Pain

Pearl Bay

Robinson Pt

Sav Isl

N

0   0.5   1.0 mile

Cooper Bay

Cooper Pt

Start

STATE

needed to cut lumber for buildings, grist mills were needed to make flour, and so on. The mills provided not only the raw materials for settlement but also the commercial activity that the communities needed to grow and prosper. Grand Isle differed in that only one mill was erected here, and no significant manufacturing economy ever developed. The reason for this was the lack of water power, a phenomenon caused by the flat terrain and few sizable streams. Instead, the settlers turned to agriculture, and today Grand Isle continues its agricultural tradition with a number of large dairy farms as well as fruit and vegetable production.

0.0 Begin at the gate to the Grand Isle State Park, facing out of the park with Lake Champlain to your back. Proceed straight ahead for a couple hundred feet to the four-way intersection and turn RIGHT onto East Shore Road.

0.4 Continue STRAIGHT past a road on the left.

1.1 Here the road turns to pavement.

1.5 Continue past the Cedar Point Road on the right.

1.8 Bear LEFT past Tebo Terrace on the right.

2.2 Turn RIGHT onto US 2, heading north, and pass the Chamberlin Sunset Farm on the right and a large cemetery across the road on your left.

3.0 Turn RIGHT onto the road across from the Grand Isle Store.

3.4 Bear LEFT around the corner as the road turns once more to dirt, and pass Pearl Bay on your right.

4.2 Bend sharply to the RIGHT past a road going to the left.

5.1 Pass the Savage Island Farm sign and mailbox.
Savage Island is located about a mile and a half off shore, and you can see it over your shoulder to the right. Named after the Mr. Savage who originally surveyed much of Grand Isle, this privately owned, two hundred-acre island is a working sheep farm. Owner Ted Riehl raises more than one hundred Montadale sheep, a breed noted for their ability to thrive when required to forage for feed. Island farming presents a new set of challenges that the hillside farmer never encounters. Transportation to the mainland is unpredictable for several weeks of the year, for the thin ice of late winter and early spring makes both boating through the water and driving over the ice impossible.

6.1 Pass the Phelps-Wright farm, and follow the road as it bends to the left.

6.6 Turn RIGHT.

8.1 Pass a sign for the Point Farm on your right as the road begins to head inland away from the lake.

8.4 Turn LEFT onto US 2 and begin traveling south.

9.9 Turn RIGHT, just past the Den of Antiquity antiques business.

11.1 Continue STRAIGHT past this four-way intersection, with the road stretching straight ahead before you.

11.8 Continue STRAIGHT past a road on your left.

12.4 Bear LEFT and begin traversing the western side of the island. New York State and the Andirondack Mountains are visible on the far side of the lake.

Offshore to the right is Young Island, a beautiful small island with interesting geological characteristics, a variety of vegetation, and a nesting habitat for Vermont's endangered crowned night heron.

With the exception of the Great Lakes, Lake Champlain is the largest freshwater lake in the United States. It is 108-miles long, up to 12 miles in width, and covers 490 square miles. Its greatest depth is 490 feet. The lake is 100 feet above sea level, and the magnificent Adirondacks that form its backdrop to the west rise nearly a mile above it.

13.8   Continue STRAIGHT onto a paved road, passing a road on your left and then the Lake Farm Nursery on your right.

14.6   Continue STRAIGHT past a road on your left.

15.7   Turn LEFT onto a dirt road across from the entrance to the ferry dock. The ferry runs regularly from here to Plattsburgh, New York, leaving every twenty minutes and taking twelve minutes to cross the lake.

16.7   Turn RIGHT.

17.8   Turn LEFT onto US 2.

Much of Grand Isle's beauty is a result of a shoreline that to date has escaped extensive development.

17.9 Turn RIGHT onto the Grand Isle State Park access road.

18.7 Continue STRAIGHT through the four-way intersection at which you turned at the trip's beginning.

18.8 You've reached the starting point.

Accommodations

Charlie's Northland Lodge, Box 88, US 2, North Hero, VT 05474 (802–372–8822). With unmatched views of the lake and distant mountains, this is a great place from which to launch cycling expeditions as well as fishing, sailing, canoeing, or tennis activities. Housekeeping cottages available upon request.

North Hero House, P.O. Box 106, North Hero, VT 05474 (802–372–8237). Abundant, delicious food, gracious hospitality, and fine accommodations are the trademarks of this intimate island inn overlooking Lake Champlain.

Camping

Grand Isle State Park, Grand Isle, VT 05458.
Picnic tables and fireplaces, swimming, fishing, boating, boat rentals, tent sites, lean-tos, trailer sites, hot showers, rec building.

Bicycle Service

Earle's Schwinn Cyclery, 2500 Williston Road, S. Burlington, VT (802–864–9197); 135 Main Street, Burlington, VT (802–862–4203). Sales and service.

Essex Junction Bicycles, 50 Pearl Street, Essex Jct., VT (802–878–1275).

Island Cyclery, RR 1 Box 557, South Hero, VT (802–372–6619).

Jericho Sports, 7 LaFayette Drive, RR 1 Box 14, Jericho, VT (802–899–3549).

Kevin Smith's Sport Connection, 38 S. Main, St. Albans, VT (802–868–2511). Sales and service.

North Star Cyclery, 100 Main Street, Burlington, VT (802–863–3832).

The Ski Rack Bike Shop, 81 Main Street, Burlington, VT (802–658–3313). Sales and service.

Victory Sports, 76 Heineberg Drive, Colchester, VT (802–862–0963).

Winooski Bicycle Shop, 12 W. Canal Street, P.O. Box 152, Winooski, VT (802–655–3233).

Also from Backcountry Publications and Countryman Press

Backcountry Publications and Countryman Press, long known for fine books on travel and outdoor recreation, offer a range of practical and readable guides. These carefully prepared books feature detailed trail and tour directions, notes on points of interest and natural highlights, maps and photographs.

Biking Series
25 Bicycle Tours on Delmarva, $9.95
25 Bicycle Tours in Eastern Pennsylvania, Second Edition $8.95
20 Bicycle Tours in the Finger Lakes, Second Edition $9.95
20 Bicycle Tours in the Five Boroughs (New York City), $8.95
25 Bicycle Tours in the Hudson Valley, $9.95
25 Bicycle Tours in Maine, Second Edition $9.95
30 Bicycle Tours in New Hampshire, Third Edition $10.95
25 Bicycle Tours in New Jersey, $9.95
20 Bicycle Tours in and around New York City, $7.95
25 Bicycle Tours in Ohio's Western Reserve, $11.95
25 Bicycle Tours in Southern Indiana, $10.95
25 Bicycle Tours in Vermont, Second Edition $9.95
25 Bicycle Tours in and around Washington, D.C., $9.95
25 Mountain Bike Tours in Massachusetts, $9.95
25 Mountain Bike Tours in Vermont, $9.95

Guides to Vermont
25 Ski Tours in Vermont, $8.95
Canoe Camping Vermont & New Hampshire Rivers, Second Edition $8.95
Fifty Hikes in Vermont, Fourth Edition $11.95
Family Resorts of the Northeast, $12.95
New England's Special Places, $12.95
Walks & Rambles in the Upper Connecticut River Valley, $9.95

Our travel and outdoor recreation guides are available through bookstores and specialty shops. For a free catalog write: The Countryman Press, Inc., Dept. APB, PO Box 175, Woodstock, VT 05091.